SIMPLE SELF HELP

Finding your own way

NICK STURGEON

Bridgewater Ink

Special thanks to:
Henry Piper, Ray & Cathy Harris, Bette Mandino, Paul Hatchwell and Carlos Castaneda.

To My Best Boys: Henry and Johnny
I have learned different and uniquely helpful lessons from each of you and hope that I have given and shared a part of who I am with you in return.
This dedication comes to you with my grateful thanks for you being a part of the team that has allowed us to have adventures, learn from mistakes and to create our very own very best life.

Contents

Foreword

Simple Self Help is an encouragement to you to engage fully in your life and the experiences, opportunities and lessons that it brings to you.

Rather than expect that "one day" or "someday" you will have what you want, start by allowing yourself to see your life for what it is today. Remember that this day is all you have since you cannot guarantee tomorrow or bask in past glory days. Start now. Doing this one day at a time will also give you a greater sense of being involved in your own life and bring you into the moment as things happen. Every day is a new opportunity to choose the way you want things to be, allowing you to say Yes or No to the many experiences on offer.

Simple Self Help contains many different ideas about how you can influence what you want in your life, for the better. I hope that it also provides you with scope for instruction, lesson and reflection on how you can live each day.

Enjoy yourself.

Nick

Introduction

The more choice that each of us exercise in our lives, the more we get to choose from the better quality options that keep presenting themselves. You can develop strategies and approaches that work for you and allow you to make better quality decisions over how you either spend or invest your time.

Recognizing and Welcoming Synchronicity

This whole process of synchronicity, or having the right people and the right opportunities or lessons appear in your life at the most appropriate time, is a part of what this book is about. I want to provide you with a resource that you can use at the pace that suits you best on a given day.

I know for myself there are days when I have every good intention to create something I am pleased with, to accomplish a task I have been putting off for a while, but things turn out flatter than I expected or the outcome of an action was different to what I had envisioned. The amazing thing is that when I stop trying hard to make something perfect and instead enjoy what I love doing, or when I let go of what the outcome has to feel like, then the day turns out to be great and the energy is just perfect.

Life will not only give you what you focus on, but it will also provide you with the solutions and the most impeccable timings for your circumstances.

Let me share an example. I was out with my family as we looked for a new house because we had decided to sell our home and move to a village nearby. We parked the car close to the house we wanted to look at and stepped out to have a look at it. At the same moment we did this, some neighbors came by and spoke with us about the property, the vendors, the local schools, and quickly dealt with many of the questions that the realtor had been unable to answer.

In another situation, a client had called me about wanting to increase the revenue and profits from her business. What she was doing with her business was new to me in terms of a product range, but the facts of branding, developing a product profile, wrapping the benefits, marketing a consistent message and converting prospects into actual clients were the same that many businesses go through. On the day she raised her questions with me, I received a call from an existing client who had already gone through the same issues with an almost identical product range I had been unaware of. I was able to put the two in touch and the first client had her answers faster than she had imagined possible.

Hold onto the Intention

There will be times you choose to read a whole

section of this book. At other times, you will pick up the book and trust you will be given the page that you need at the exact moment. This is fine also. Having the intention to get what you need from this book as a resource at the right time is what trust is all about.

There will be aspects of your life right now that are calling out for your attention and focus. You have no idea of how you will heal the hurt, deal with the pain, or discover the solutions that you think you need without comprehending how you will find the answer. But the answers, the solutions and the healing are all here. It is all around you right now. Trusting that you will have it revealed to you, or explained for you, is all you need to be aware of.

Enjoy the Ride

The sharing here is from my heart and from that part of me that I have tried not to rule or to discipline too much, instead letting the words come as they will when I am patient with them.

This book has grown beyond my original idea of answering the various questions that people have frequently raised with me, or which I have found myself asking aloud at various times of my life. It is here for you as a gift of words, providing you with the opportunity to find answers to questions you have and resolutions to issues you may not have known required attention.

I want you to enjoy the content and feel totally free to flip from chapter to chapter or dip into the topic that is important for you right now. Simple self Help is for you.

Nick

1

YOUR ENVIRONMENT

Be there more often

I fully realize that the life I lead now as a writer is one that came about as a direct result of goals and dreams that I had from childhood. However, when I heard the stories of authors and others who shared their ideas with the world, it never occurred to me that I would have to spend quite some time on the road. Maybe I should have crystallized my vision of what my life should be like and kept out the commuting!

Nothing used to make me sadder than my first born son on the telephone saying *"Are you coming home tonight, Daddy?"* and him not grasping the fact that I was five hours, or even five hundred miles away. Or being unavailable to my family when they needed me for a school sports day or an evening social event with new friends.

No hotel room offers real comfort, just a brief respite from the travelling and a place where you can collect your thoughts in peace. Of course, you can be attracted to and even seduced by the hotels and the restaurants and the sense of being looked after by people who are simply doing their job when they serve you, but so what? What difference does it make to your life that you receive good service in a hotel, but you miss a child's birthday? Or you don't get to attend the Parent and Teacher evening, or a special anniversary? All because of a schedule, meeting or travel requirement imposed by something beyond your control.

Getting home to be greeted by family is always a joy, even if they are unsure when you might be going away again. If in doubt, get home soon. You never get this time again with those you love.

Make a commitment to yourself to enjoy the time with those you love and then spend as much time as possible doing just that. Nothing else. I am not going to suggest you make a radical change to your work or profession in order to spend more of your time in alignment with what you believe in and what your values are. But I *will* ask you to work out your beliefs and your values and to ask yourself if you are even close to them in your day-to-day activity.

Memories are made and created by the way that you live your life moment by moment, so use the moments of today to build a picture you will look back on with love and gratitude.

Seek out the people who want to be with you and spend as much time as you can in their company. Each of you will always be grateful that this is what you chose to do. Your regrets will be less when you look back on these times. And by the way, these times are the only ones you have.

Make your home a place of replenishment and renewal

It is so easy to see your home as simply the place where you sleep before heading out into the world. Instead, look at it with the same eyes you had when you were excited about moving in, remembering the joy you felt when you browsed through the brochure.

Whether you live in an apartment, a back-to-back house or a penthouse, this is where you are right now. You could be in a place you love, or you may be in one that leaves you with the feeling that you need to move on to something better. What matters is that either the whole space or a particular part of it is dedicated to being special for you.

Create a special place in your living room, decorate it just the way you want, hang great pictures around the property that inspire you. Find a corner you can fill with special photos, pictures, artwork or decorations that have positive meaning for you.

My own study is my special place at the bottom of our garden. My desk top was once the door of our shed, the surface grained and weather worn. One wall is covered with fabulous cards displaying inspiring quotes. Pictures of friends smile at me from the walls.

The last thing you want to create is a mental picture of your home as a place of burden, debt and mortgage repayment! It is so much more fun and more practical to see it as the source of inspiration and place to rebuild yourself before venturing out into the world. And the biggest irony of all is this: the less you focus on the things you don't want, the more you get what works for you and pleases you!

Create a space that will nurture you and allow you to be supported to do and achieve the things you seek, and to be the person you were born to be.

Be IN the room!

Have you ever had your partner speaking to you and you did not hear a word because you were thinking about something, worrying about a job, or considering the work for the next day? I can't believe you if you say you haven't been there! I've been there too often: I've read the book, seen the movie and bought the T-shirt on this one! We get sidetracked by something when we are supposedly doing something else.

This simple and very powerful concept has made such a difference. *"Be IN the room"* means exactly this. When you are with someone, give them your focus. This is the most important thing you have for someone else at the time.

If you are working on a project, make it the only thing you are doing for that allocated time.

If you are teaching your kid to ride a bicycle, then you are teaching your kid to ride a bicycle. You are not answering your mobile or composing an email in your head.

If I am writing this page for you, then I am writing this page for you. I am not thinking about making a drink, going through my post, seeing my children, watching a film, walking into the village or paying a credit card bill. I am writing this page. Just writing this page. Nothing else.

In another moment I can choose to sit by the pool, walk along the beach for an hour, or make a drink and sit by the fire on a cool afternoon.

Distraction can take us away from the moment we are in. It will prevent you from being present at some of the most magical, wonderful and touching moments of life, unless you recognize it and refuse to give it power.

Get yourself present in this moment and this place where you are. By letting your mind wander to other places, other things and commitments, you lose the benefit that comes from appreciating your current circumstances and situations. If losing the focus on where you are now takes away from your current experience, then get back in the game immediately. Be IN the room. It will make a huge difference that you will notice straight away.

You will also be aware that people notice your focus and appreciate it. Be here now.

Look after your home as a reflection of yourself

When you walk a friend around the house you want them to be amazed at what you have done with the space, intrigued by how you have created special places. Make your home an investment in allowing yourself to be your best, so that whether you are home with your family or out there in the world doing whatever you do, you do it from a place of replenishment and strength.

Create and then protect your environment so that it

nurtures and supports you in being truly yourself. Do whatever is necessary in terms of decoration, ornaments, attractive features, views, artwork, etc., to make the place a special one which will lift and inspire you. Your home space, whether a bedroom in a shared house, or a property of your own, is your own opportunity to create a true reflection of who you are.

If you need candles and music to relax, then don't delay in buying them. But only bring home the ones that give you what you need.

If you feel better writing to friends on good-quality traditional stationery instead of knocking out a quick email, then visit a stationery store, select a pen that you love and develop a special place for your writing and correspondence. This is a part of who you are and reflects a way that you can express yourself. Shortcuts are most often the ones that get you lost!

Likewise, if you want to have the company of friends around for a special celebration of who you are and why they are important to you, then book a date in the diary and get the invites out!

On the downside of having your home as a reflection of yourself, are there any hidden - or plainly obvious - messages around the property that stare back at you? I am thinking of the clutter, rubbish, junk and other mess that has been allowed to accumulate.

Try these areas to find things that may be past their best times:

- Your wardrobe
- Your desk

- Wherever you keep your personal financial statements
- Your garage
- The attic or loft, or perhaps the cupboard under the stairs

You will find things you thought you had lost, and even more things you wish had disappeared! Throw away those items that have no function, don't fit, have little value, and which you might never use again. If you insist on getting something in return, then take it all to a car-boot sale, place small ads in your local paper, or get yourself an account with an online auction website and get some money for it.

A client told me of how she had finally thrown away the historic credit card bills of when she had been horribly in debt and which she held onto as a sign of the troubles she had overcome. Yet by refusing to throw these away for years, she had actually been reinforcing the feelings of debt, owing people, and agonizing about an uncertain income. Within a few short months of throwing away this negative junk, she began to enjoy regular income for the first time in years.

What is the outside of your home like for you and those who visit? This is so important given that if you work outside the house, it is the last impression when you leave and the first you see when you return at the end of the day. How does your pathway welcome you? What about the windows of your home?

Does the entrance reflect clarity and order, or chaos and uncertainty?

Are the images you hang on your walls ones that lift and motivate you or do you hang onto inherited items you don't want, but are afraid to give away?

Does the first room of the house fill you with positive images or drag you down mentally?

Let go of the rubbish, the clutter and the junk and make space for more and better things to come into your life. Life will amaze you!

2

CHOOSE YOUR THINKING

The saying *"What you see is what you get"* is just as true for your speech. Self-talk, or what you say when speaking to yourself, is the process of helping you change your results through changing the quality of your thoughts. How you comment on life has a way of bouncing back on you.

Think about the words that come out of your mouth and the thoughts you have. Little by little, improve the quality of them, stop using critical language, and start to create positive images in your mind. Reflect on good outcomes for your projects and begin to visualize the best results that are possible.

Speak well of yourself and others, of their ability and yours. Guess what? You will get what you see consistently in your mind's eye. Start to see good things happening and they will.

Try these simple and clear affirmations or statements of intent and watch what happens in your life:

"I am having a good day and great things are happening for me."

"My life works."

"I respect myself and my behavior and this gets me great results in all I do."

"Applying my natural talents to the tasks in front of me allows me to be successful."

"By identifying and choosing the results I want to achieve, I am likely to do the work necessary to get those same results."

"My connection to my intuition and abilities is sufficient to create productive and successful outcomes in the goals that are truly important to me."

"I like myself."

"If it's to be, it's up to me."

Since your own mind is the one that you spend most of your time conversing with, it makes perfect sense for you to speak with yourself in a way that is loving, appreciative and supportive.

A friend wrote me about how she had been experiencing hard times. Her personal finances were a mess and she could not get any increase in earnings at work. At home, she and her partner were frequently arguing over things that were almost always inconsequential and yet causing big fights between them.

By taking the time to reflect on her own thoughts and the inner conversation she was having with herself, she was able to see that the words and language she had been using were largely self-critical. Around the subject of work and advancement within the company, she had been thinking that her co-workers were better qualified and better skilled than she was, effectively downplaying her own talent and ability. In her private life, she was holding onto thoughts about her and her partner having nothing in common, and not being interested in any joint pastimes or activities.

Over a period of months she began to gently monitor her thoughts and the self-talk, inserting new phrases that helped her to recognize and acknowledge her skills in the workplace and the contribution she was capable of making at home. In her relationship, she started to introduce more self-talk about her love for her partner and for his appreciation of her. Over time the friction between them lessened to the point that they were able to enjoy each other's company again and develop their relationship to where they each wanted it to be.

The way you think and the quality or direction of those thoughts can have such a profound direct impact on your life that you should take some time to consider how you are thinking.

Thoughts that are generally non-supportive might come though as worries, doubts or fears. More damaging still are thoughts around resentfulness, jealousy and anger. None of these can be of any real use to you and simply take your thinking away from other better trains of thought that could otherwise enhance your self-esteem, build your inner confidence and allow you to be more engaged with others on a daily basis.

Are you really able to hold onto lingering thoughts of resentment about something that did not work out for you in the past, and still engage in an active conversation with a friend in the present moment? Unlikely. So you may as well begin to look at the way your thinking is creating your reality each day, and have it working for you rather than against you.

Leave others be

Ever notice that people do stupid things that seem to hurt and distress you? Do you honestly think they do these crazy things just to get you upset? Get real! They probably don't even know half the time that you are aware of them. Do you really think that you can change them or their behavior unless they want to make the changes for themselves?

In the vast majority of situations, there is no intent to cause upset. Rather, it is all down to our own perception of the situation. Years ago when I was broken hearted that a girl had not noticed me, let alone done anything to encourage me to spend time with her, my friend Glenn put it perfectly:

"While you are sitting around at home and moping, she's out dancing."

He was right! In that instance I did not even figure in her thinking, and yet I was reacting to nothing and imagining the worst of everything. Who was suffering in this ridiculous one-sided "pity party" way of thinking? Only me!

What good does it do you to hang onto critical thinking about other people? How much energy are you using up in holding negative and hurtful or painful thoughts about someone? Someone might actually be a jerk. Is it going to have much impact on your life? Not unless you let it. Let them go. Free up some space in your mind and your heart for other, better things to come in. You do want something better, don't you?

Other people's stuff is just that: it's theirs. It is not yours. One of the quickest ways to get yourself stressed out is to judge that:

a) what someone else does or how they lead their life is wrong, and

b) that it is your mission to either do something about it or to be affected by it.

Likewise, if you have found yourself imposing pain and upset on others and are aware of doing it, then stop now. What right do you have to create this pain and hassle for them?

Closer to home, what good is it doing you anyway? What is the payback or benefit you get from expending your energy this way?

I doubt you will see a single benefit worth holding on to and suggest you look in the mirror and let go of this behavior. Immediately.

You might just end up being happier and less stressed. That's what you can call a result!

Self-education

The best money you can ever spend is money invested on your own mind, expanding the quality of your knowledge and increasing your ability to take control of your circumstances or make new ones that work better for you. Whether it is attending an evening class, going on a weekend seminar, listening to podcasts, learning via the internet or simply browsing in your local library or used book store, you are giving yourself new information.

My friend Ian once said to me that *"If you read for one hour a day on a topic where you are a novice, within a year you will become incredibly competent in that topic and within two years become an expert."* I dare you to try and prove us both wrong.

Pick something you want to know more about:

- Climbing Out of Debt
- Building your own Home
- Cooking with Pasta
- Investing in Real Estate
- Being with your Kids
- Painting with Oils
- Repairing your Car
- Growing Roses

Whatever it is, you make the choice of topic and put in the work. Your mind will take care of absorbing the learning.

Join a class, get into a discussion group, contribute your thoughts to a book club, and meet with the people who can teach you new skills and insights. You will be astounded at the power of your mind to expand to new learning.

Start this process by beginning with something you are curious about learning more about. Once you have enjoyed the fruits of this learning, pick a topic that might help you in a work-related skill, in your home life, or in building your skills with other people, and watch your progress.

Go to the art gallery. Book yourself on a course in archaeology or ancient history. Buy yourself a session in a life drawing class or a series of flying lessons. Start to learn the basics of a new language. Join an outdoors club where you can learn map reading and fieldcraft. Commit to doing any of these new things because you want to follow your curiosity and satisfy an urge to learn more about something.

Remember this piece of wisdom:

"A skill once learned can never be taken away, and your mind can never go back to the time before you gained the new knowledge."

Personal effectiveness

You have just one life and this comprises thousands of single days. Lots of people are efficient at "time management" but dreadfully ineffective personally. Time management is not the answer.

You need to decide what you are looking to do each day and have a plan for this the night before. Make a simple list of the things ahead of you. This is easy enough. Then prioritize them according to your values and what is important to you. It is this step that takes the thoughtfulness, but which then gives you a list of tasks and activities that will make you effective in a powerful way.

Effectiveness means cutting through the everyday "stuff" that turns up in your diary and in-box, and getting on with what matters to you and what will really make a difference for you.

My former neighbor, Simon, is a complete wizard at dealing with paperwork and email. I once invited him over to the house to help me take back control of my desk. Not only did we go through a ton of papers, files, letters, magazines, articles, bills, and emails, but we threw so much of it away that I was amazed.

We did the same with the contents of my filing cabinets and ended up getting money for the office furniture and storage that was no longer needed. I had been hanging on to information in case I might one day need it.

I was rather scared at throwing out all this "stuff" I had accumulated. Guess what he said to me?

"If it was really important, the people who sent it can let you have another version and most of them could even send it to you electronically and do away with the mass of paper."

What you will be doing from this moment on is a result of choosing where you focus your attention. I dislike the phrase "attention management" and suggest instead you just get on with it. This is Simple Self Help in action.

Rather than being driven by the time-bound calendar approach, consider assessing what needs to be done on the basis of your values, your choices, and the things that make your life the exciting journey it is for you. For example, what five things do you want to accomplish this month in each of your main Life Roles? These roles are easy to identify and might be as a Parent, Friend, Partner,

Staff Member, Hobbyist, or Saver. Choose just a few things that you would like to see achieved this month in each role and commit these to paper.

Measure your effectiveness by whether you are moving forward with the projects of importance to you. If not, trim out some of the unnecessary "stuff."

Visualization

While knowing what you want is a useful skill in life and a great way of to move things forward and to improve your circumstances, there is a vast difference between knowing this logically and with using visualization as a means of bringing the emotions of that circumstance closer to you.

To really feel and see and be in the picture of how you want your situation to be is a greatly more powerful way forward.

For many years I struggled enormously with my moods, allowing the feelings of guilt and shame from my past, the untaken opportunities, and the regretted behaviors to cause me pain and great sadness. I allowed this baggage and the discomfort to come along with me each day, permitting the past to not only distort but even damage the present moment that I was in. It sometimes felt as though I was not only allowing the past to come with me, but that I was almost inviting it to join me for the day! Can you imagine yourself doing anything so silly as encouraging a group of people you either dislike, find uncomfortable to be around or simply cannot bear, to be with you for hours at a time and at your own request? No, of course not! So don't drag your past around anymore.

I talked with friends who had taken steps to transition from a difficult emotional place they did not want to be in, to gradually moving into a space that was more supportive, more true to who they really were. They explained that a significant part of their own improvement had come from the act of foreseeing or envisioning the situation that they wanted to create for themselves.

A friend who was constantly struggling with unfulfilled relationships began to create a picture in his mind of himself and a beautiful woman who would understand him, share her dreams with him, and with whom he could develop a safe and loving relationship. Over a period of several months of working with this picture, he attracted several good women into his life, and eventually chose one with whom he entered into a truly loving relationship. In this new relationship he found himself feeling safe and cherished for the first time in his adult life.

In another situation, I knew a young couple who were living in a cramped first floor apartment in the city, making barely enough each month to cover their rent and utility bills. They wanted desperately to make the break to the suburbs where they felt they could spend the same amount of money on a small house with a garden. Keen to start a family together, but unsure that the city was the right place for them to bring up a child in such shabby surroundings, they were encouraged to work with visualizing the kind of place they wanted to be in.

They began to cut pictures of living spaces, homes

and gardens from magazines, and collect postcards, street scenes of small communities, and any images that they felt represented the sort of place they wanted to move to. They placed the pictures on several notice boards around their apartment and kept their faith that the Universe would support them in their goal.

A month into the building of their Dream Boards, the woman received a call from a friend at work. She was ringing to ask if they wanted to look at a house in a beautiful semi-rural community on the outskirts of the city. It belonged to a family member who wanted either to sell or to rent the place out. They jumped at the chance to see the place and inspect it for themselves. When they got there, it was precisely what they wanted and the living room and garden were virtually identical to two of the pictures they had been envisioning and working with that past month!

Visualizing what you want means putting yourself in a place emotionally and mentally where you can see in your mind's eye the ideal outcome that you want to attract.

It differs from goal setting as a process but builds upon that activity. By creating the picture, you are involving more senses than just thought. The visual image involves your sight. Putting yourself physically in the place you imagine allows you to engage your physical senses of touch, sound, and even taste as you imagine and visualize yourself in that place, that circumstance, that opportunity. While you are there, you can allow your emotions to complete the picture by feeling what it is like to be there and to have the sensations all around you.

Begin to visualize today. Start with something small that you would like to have happen or which you would like to attract. Notice the feelings you associate with that outcome being achieved and allow yourself to explore how good it feels to have this happening for you.

3

YOUR MONEY

Face the reality of it

This is a topic we all have so many thoughts and perspectives on. It is something that so few of us ever learn at school or from our family when growing up. I mean, how are you supposed to get a financial role-model from a worker (whether schoolteacher, driver, banker, barman, chef or pilot, farmer or coastguard) who is just surviving on a salary that provides only enough for them to pay their own bills, let alone develop your own savings and patterns of financial independence? How do you just come out and ask someone about their approach to investing for the future?

We have to learn about it now and we have to get on with it. Every month that you refuse to acknowledge and learn the basic principles of financial success and money management is another month wasted, and another lot of compound interest missing from your savings or investments. The best way to learn money management is to start right now—not next week, next month, or next year.

Simply deciding to face up to the subject of money and the emotion that it brings up, can be a strong and positive start to dealing with the subject. An example of facing money as a topic might be something as straightforward as opening an envelope that arrives and which you know contains a bill. Once you get the bill out you are in a position to file it and set a date for it to get paid.

Keep a running file of the amounts you owe and track the money you have coming in. When it comes to handling and managing money, your conscious awareness is nine-tenths of the reason for your success. The less you know about your financial situation, and the more you deny needing to own and control the detail, the more likely it is that you will struggle to attract money into your life and keep yourself on solid financial footing.

The last thing you should do is leave the post until another day or until you think you might have some cash to pay it. By opening the post and dealing with it, you are starting to put yourself in better control of the situation.

Being aware of your numbers is one of the keys to understanding and being in control of your finances. If you are bringing in enough money, you can meet your bills and save. If you know your numbers each day, then you will also know when it is time to turn up the energy and attract more money into your life.

Earning it

Money will come to you to the extent that you offer a service that is of value. Of course, you could marry money, inherit money or even win it on the lottery, but the reality is that any of those methods involves you in some processes you might regret later!

The greater the value you offer, the greater the inflow of money. If you ever find yourself thinking you are earning less money than you are worth, then look at your contribution to service. When people know that you offer something of value, they will turn up in droves to hand over their money.

Receiving money can be as simple as asking for it in the first place! When was the last time you actually stopped racing around and said aloud *"I need more money and welcome it now"*, instead of simply spending hours worrying about the lack of money you were experiencing at the time?

For whatever reason, it is very easy to push away money and for often the same reasons that we push away so much of the goodness and the riches that life has to offer us. The reason we push it away is because we are unable to receive with ease and without guilt. So the more time you can put into receiving with pleasure and to saying *"Thank You"* for all the abundance that the Universe has to offer you, the more likely it is that you will start to notice some great things turning up in your life.

Being able to receive is crucial to your earning money, and you will turn opportunities away until you can receive without concern or without worry. Simply receive in the moment.

If you are experiencing lack of inflow and plenty of outflow, you need to reverse the trend. The simplest way is for you to review and reflect upon the value of the work you do and the people you deliver it to.

What skills can you offer?

How about a level of service, support or problem solving?

What are you good at naturally that your friends and co-workers often appreciate and ask for your help with?

Could you do a skills audit of your abilities and talents, and consider too the skills of your friends and family?

Look at the amount of money that these skills and talents can be worth in the right market place. Notice that I said *"the RIGHT market place."* Having the right talents applied to the wrong market, to the wrong audience group, or to the wrong potential client, will have no value as you will have missed the mark.

Get Creative over your ability to earn and to attract money. Start with something simple and develop from this level upwards. Take an example such as manifesting or attracting to you a cup of coffee or a big smile from someone on the street. Once you have managed this and proven to yourself how easy it can be to receive what you put out for, then you can move onto bigger and better things and situations.

The same is true for money. You might begin with saying to yourself *"I am attracting the funds needed to pay for my car maintenance"* and then let go of any attachment to the outcome. All manner of things could happen to get you the desired end result of having the car maintenance bill settled. It could be that someone gives you the money as a gift, or you receive a tax credit for a matching amount of money, or maybe you find a windfall to the same amount. What matters is that you ask for the result and let the money make its own way to you.

To attract money from your job, or a small business that you choose to set up and run, first decide what service you will offer and then commit to delivering that service. Invest time and energy in identifying the buyers for your skills, services, products and talents. Make it *Your Business* to be *In Business* with these buyers.

In the context of your job, invest your energies in becoming a valuable resource for the business that employs you. Learn more about your niche and develop your skills in such a way as to make you more important to the success of the company. This might be through online learning, attending in-house training events, or simply through getting involved within your local business community.

As your work-related learning and abilities grow, it is very likely that this will be matched with greater opportunities and benefits that can be measured in terms of reward and money.

When this happens be ready for it, and make sure that you take those rewards to the bank!

Keeping it

This one is really easy.

To hold onto your money, spend it at slower rate than it comes in. Now, was that rocket science? Hardly! But most people have no idea how they spend their money. Slow down the pace at which it leaves your account or moves through your hands.

I suggest that you grab a sheet of paper and take it everywhere you go for a whole week. Use it to record every single penny, peso, dime, dollar, shekel, and euro you spend. Keep every receipt and write everything down. Do the same again the second and the third and fourth weeks until you have a One Month pattern of your Spending and Inflow.

By totting up the numbers on your sheet for each week and deducting this money from your weekly or monthly income, you know exactly where you stand financially each month. And all you have to do to win at the money game is take an area of your regular expenditure, work out what this is as a percentage of your income and ensure that next month you spend a reduced portion of your income in this area.

To start winning, you either Increase your income or reduce your expenditure. If your income is fixed, but you reduce your expenditure, then you will be ahead of the game and you can choose to enhance the quality of your life by spending on some better things, or you can place the surplus into a savings account.

If you can increase your income and maintain the same fixed costs you can do the same again and place more money aside into an account where you get the rewards for having done so.

Where you can do both, i.e. increase your income and reduce your fixed costs, then you are in control of a very positive move forward, maintaining a lifestyle you choose and placing cash in the savings program for your benefit further down the road.

Wherever and whenever you start, enjoy the process and realize that through the decision to keep track of your money you put yourself in a position of being able to keep hold of the money for the long term. So get proactive and start to monitor all the money that comes your way. By knowing what you have and where it goes, you get to choose how you spend what you hang on to.

Paying down debt

The first and most obvious rule here is not to get into debt in the first place.

However, given the ease with which shops and retailers offer credit to all who they deal with, it is easy to collect plenty of personal debt seemingly without trying too hard. If you are already working with debt in your life then you need to take action to reduce it.

Understand exactly how much money you owe. Draw up a comprehensive list of all the companies and people you owe money to. Be honest with yourself in doing this process. Open every envelope that is sent by the people you owe money to. Keep them all in one file and in a place where you can find it quickly. Stay in regular communication with your creditors (your creditor is the person who has given you credit as opposed to a debtor, who is someone owing you money), and let them know what is happening - even when you have no money - and nothing is happening to reduce the amount that you owe.

Get clear on the numbers and you can be clear on your options.

Dealing with the bills and the debts that you have is traditionally best done with a focus on the interest rates that are highest. Split your available funds for debt repayment such that you are making the greatest inroads on the ones that are costing you the most.

A contrary view and one that I adopted early on, is simply to start by clearing the smallest debt first. Pay this one down in full and get the buzz of success. Pay the next one off and now you have two completely cleared debts, paid in full. Continue the process and reduce the number of debtors and of course the volume of the debt you owe.

Keep a strict and accurate handle on the paperwork related to your debt situation and ensure that you stay away from other opportunities to waste money. Your priority is to deal with the existing debt and reduce it down to nothing, however long this task takes you.

Making it work for you - saving

Albert Einstein apparently described the way that you can make money from the interest on your savings as the "eighth wonder of the world". He was talking about the miracle of compound interest.

He was justified in his excitement about the way the bank will give you extra money for allowing them to keep your money on deposit. They will lend your money to other people who have become borrowers, and in exchange will reward you with a percentage increase on your own initial money. The money they give you is the result of compound interest.

The sooner you can put some money aside, the better. If you can then add a regular amount - no matter how small - to your savings, you will see your money grow time and time again over the years. This is the principle of money working for you whether you are working, sleeping or playing.

You can start by trying to save an amount from your earnings each month. This amount can be the same each paycheck, or it's even easier to go for a percentage of each check. No matter how much you earn or bring in each pay period, if you tell yourself that you are going to save 5% or 10%, you will always be able to calculate the amount you need to deposit into your savings.

Get into this habit of paying yourself first. It will always stand you in good order and create the growth of the savings.

If you allow yourself to think that you should pay your bills and your expenses first and intend to save what is left - guess what - there will be nothing left.

But if you do set aside that 10% from everything you receive before you look at the bills, you have the comfort of knowing you already have 10% set aside as savings for the long term. And almost by magic the 90% that you have left for everything else seems to expand and to grow such that you do not miss the 10% you have already put safely away for your future.

Get started now and you will love what it does for you. Enjoy knowing the pleasure of having a consistently growing nest egg for your future, and one which is within your own control and has been structured through your own diligence and wisdom. Each time you get a dividend or interest check, take some of the money and spend it on a treat for yourself, re-investing the majority remaining so that your balance continues to grow and bring more benefit.

Increasing it - investment

As you develop the powerful habits of spending less than you earn, of accumulating savings, and earning interest on those savings, then you might over a longer timescale, consider investing a small percentage in a business or venture of some sort. Personally, I find investing in other companies to be difficult if they are really small because so much depends upon the character and determination of the founder or owner of the business.

With a small business investment you can be very vulnerable to making a mistake, seduced by the money or the possibility of a quick profit. Too often the entrepreneurial energy can attract the interest of investors who seek a fast result and, in doing so, people can drop their guard and forget or overlook the need for a little investigation and due diligence.

If you are considering investing in a small business then it might well be one that you start and run yourself, which will also give you the tax benefits that come with business ownership. Give this a lot of thought. If it doesn't grab you and hold your interest, then stay away from owning a small business and simply consider the investment route as being potentially better for your lifestyle and character. Consider investment opportunities in more established businesses; one could be a good home for a portion of the savings you have accumulated for yourself.

If the idea of a business of your own is simply too much to contemplate - either because it is such a new concept or possibly because it is too frightening - then placing a portion of your savings into stocks and shares is likely to be a slightly safer return on your money.

You have the benefit that you can maintain an interest in public companies through the internet and online articles, following the stories behind each company and the sectors they are active in. This way you get to develop investment behavior as an interesting hobby, and the day-to-day aspects of your money are handled by those who do this for a living, which will give you a reasonable return without the hassle or angst of you needing to get involved.

Looking beyond equities and stocks, I have personally always preferred the long-term holding of residential property. That has been an easy decision for myself because people always need somewhere to live and for many years I have supplied good homes for them to rent. Buying property need not be a complicated process, and there are plenty of great online and printed materials for you to develop your skills in this sector. Just like stocks and shares, you can let someone else do the letting and managing of your property for you, or you can choose instead to upgrade your skills and manage the place yourself. You can also drive past the property and check it is still there whenever you want to!

A further route I would like to re-visit is combining some of the above approaches, but with a small or part-time venture of your own. You can choose to intentionally design your new business working from home, online, part-time or full-time, according to the results you want to create.

Sell or be sold

Running a business of your own is an activity you can tailor to your available times and resources, perhaps starting with very little. If it matches your own risk profile, then start with a small sum of money and do what you can to increase the fund.

Beyond the compound interest way of investing your money, look at the simple concept that you invest a basic sum and double it, gaining yourself a 100% return. The best way to do this is always through learning to sell something.

Selling is the simplest of skills to learn at a basic level and you can choose later to get really good at it. Start by finding something that you like enough to carry with you all the time. When someone expresses interest in it, you say, *"It's for sale. Would you like to buy it?"*

I am sure that the reason most people express a fear of selling is because they aren't comfortable waiting for the silence to be broken after asking this question.

If the person says *"Yes"*, then you have a sale. And you might have doubled your investment. If they say "*No*", then you simply go on to the next opportunity.

Do the research and see what you can invest in, for

the short, medium or long term. Again, I would recommend that you assess your approach to risk and always work within the boundaries of what is right for you.

The development of a good set of selling skills is a prerequisite to success not just in business but in a lot of personal and social situations too. Look at selling as a very useful life skill.

Learn about it

Don't think that you have to wait for life to teach you all the lessons of money education. This could take a long time! Instead get yourself enrolled on some evening classes about managing debt and credit cards, or pick up a book on the topic of saving or investing. Attend an event about starting your own business. Any of these approaches can be supported through the internet and your local evening college, so get hold of a prospectus and see what you can enroll yourself in.

Pick the brains of someone you consider to be financially sound or even successful in terms of business or money or life experience. Ask them about the mistakes they have made and how they turned various difficult situations around. You might be surprised to learn how often the person you approach will willingly give you some of their time. Often they will reveal how, for all they have achieved, there were many times when they lost it or had to start over again from scratch.

Is there someone you can invite out for lunch in order to have some of their time to discuss and consider the way you have been approaching money management?

Handling cash is another great way to learn about money. Given how much you may have become used to using plastic cards to lead your life, the use of cash will be a new experience.

I recommend you start by monitoring your finances for a while until you know what the repeated patterns of earning and spending tend to be.

Once you have done this, take from your bank enough money to last you for one week. This might be the equivalent of your week's salary, or one quarter of what you are paid in a month.

Put the money in a bowl at home and each day take the majority of the cash with you out into the world. When you have to buy something use the cash. Do this at the shops, the fuel station, coffee bars, restaurants, book stores, anywhere you buy something. The physical act of handling the money makes it more real, more present in your life.

An interesting side effect of handling the cash is that you may discover you will spend less on items that you might have unconsciously bought previously and stuck on the credit card. You may discover yourself questioning whether that drink or item of food or clothing is really worth the amount of cash the shop wants you to handover. As a result, you save the money for another day, giving yourself greater choice and more financial power.

Prosperity consciousness

Is it all in the mind? Could it really be the case that the way you think about the flow of money, and the support and resources coming to you, will either create more or less flow in your life?

If life gives you largely what you expect or what you ask for, are you asking for the right things?

Are you being clear with yourself about what you picture in your life?

Be totally conscious about what you want to see around you. Ask for those things you seek.

One of the strangest and yet simplest rules of life is that you will attract and manifest whatever it is that you think about and focus upon.

Clarify your thinking. Ask for what you want.

The Universe will support you in the achievement of your goals.

Some commentators refer to this process as Cosmic Ordering, being clear on what you want and making a request for it, almost as though you were walking around a department store filled with the choicest of goods and placing your order.

Maintaining a Prosperity Consciousness involves you being clear about what you want, and I also think it helps enormously to picture in detail the results you seek to create and to manifest.

Build strong mental pictures of the lifestyle you seek to create, of the relationships you want to draw to you, of the environment you want to work in and to live in. The greater the detail that you can picture of these circumstances you are choosing to attract, the greater the likelihood of successfully creating the reality that will be a reflection of your mental picturing.

Expectation plays a big part here also. Expect the right things to happen. Anticipate the results you have asked for coming to you and providing you with everything you require.

Create a mental picture of what you seek to have and to attract, then let go of any attachment to the outcome. The Universe will work to follow your instructions so be precise in describing what you want, and be thoughtful in the way you detail it.

Above all Prosperity Consciousness is about having the right frame of mind and the best mental energy in a positive place without distraction. This will provide you with what you need to fulfil your own mission for a life well lived.

4

YOUR FAMILY

Acknowledge them

We don't choose our parents, but we end up with them anyway! Some incredible miracle of science and biology caused you to be here. Get on with enjoying the process of living the best life that is possible for you.

You can have some siblings or none at all. You may have aunts and uncles, nephews and nieces, and long-lost cousins for all I know. See that there is a connection to these people and that you are connected to everyone else through this weird and wonderful structure called family.

Your parents and anyone else who was involved in the process of raising you performed an amazing job to bring you up in the world and contribute to the unique human being you are today. It is true that how you feel about them can either hold you back, give you strength or leave you with confusion, but they did raise you, probably when it was difficult or awkward or just downright hard work. Even if it is just an acknowledgement, you owe them something. Look out for them.

Your connection with those you love and care for can turn in a new direction. It could be a negative incident, a conversation that goes the wrong way, or some confusion that triggers a reaction other than the one you intended.

They have done good for you and allowed you to be who you are today. Take the time to acknowledge and recognize what it took to make you the amazing human being that you are. They do deserve some credit, regardless of whether you choose to spend much time with them.

We all appreciate an acknowledgement, a word of thanks, a small or a large gesture that we have done our best. This is just as true for family. Give the process some thought and then give them some of your attention.

Acknowledge the good relationships you do have. Consider how you might strengthen them, spend a little more time in them, and emotionally invest in them for the benefit of all concerned.

Make time for them

Rather than look back at life and regret the things they have done, many people regret the things they failed to do. All too often one of the items at the top of the "Wish I had done" list are things such as spend more time with my family, visit my parents, go on a trip with my brother or sister, etc. You don't really find yourself saying *"I wish I had read another report"* or *"If only I could have spent another day on work phone calls and follow-ups."*

It is a simple enough matter to put some time in your diary and see the people who are meaningful to your life, to book in with them or simply to turn up on a spur-of-the-moment impulse.

If you don't stick this time with them in the diary, it is never going to happen. Rather than neglect these important get-togethers until next year, when you will probably look back and think *"If only I had..."*, get on the phone, send them an email, write them a note and get something in the diary. None of us carry a crystal ball, or know what may happen around the corner, so get on with arranging this today.

Listen to the intuition you already have. Observe the "hunch" you get about calling someone or arranging to get together with them.

One evening after work I was heading to my home when I had the strongest feeling that I should make an effort to break off from my schedule to see my parents. It was raining and the traffic was heavy. At the end of a busy day and with a long journey ahead of me, I chose to ignore the feeling and drive on. The next day I had a call from my mother to say that my dad had just that morning suffered a massive heart attack and died suddenly.

I so wish I had listened to the message that had come to me the night before that suggested I make a turn to their village. I so keenly wish that I had gone to see my dad that night. I would have driven across the country, stayed up all night, cancelled everything just to have spent a few more hours with that wonderful man.

So take a few moments to arrange something that can

result in an hour or a day or a week together, creating memories that can then be with you always.

Just be in the moment and recognize what you do have. Realize what you can create with real time now as opposed to what you might be able to do tomorrow or the next day. Here is the thing about time: it doesn't really exist. There is only the moment that you are in now. You don't really know that tomorrow will come around on the clock.

Pick up that phone, tap on that door, hop in the car and simply arrange to enjoy the time with those you love and with those who love you. You will always have the memories of when you did something together, and that will forever be of help to you.

Stay in touch

And when you have been together with them, don't let it end there. Pick up the pieces and take responsibility for being in contact with them until the next time you manage to meet up.

"It only takes a minute" might be a great musical song, but it could just as well be the catch phrase for a person getting in touch and staying in touch.

I know that sometimes you have to grit your teeth and smile at the thought of seeing Aunty Mabel and Uncle Charlie, but guess what? You just made their day by making them feel worthwhile and special by turning up with a smile, a hug and some flowers.

With text messages and email you can act quickly on the thought about getting together and organizing something. Better still, pop into a shop in your lunch hour, buy a card, choose a nice postcard or gift and post a personal message. Heaven forbid, you could even go and visit them!

The spread of the internet and the opportunity to connect with old friends and former schoolmates or work colleagues has been an amazing gift because the click of a button can put you back in contact. When meeting up with them, either online or in person, it can be as if the intervening years never existed. You can build on the foundation of these important relationships and allow them to enrich your current life.

Further enhance the experience and the memories by getting together. It helps all of us to realize we are part of a global community that connects first and foremost at the very local and personal level.

If you doubt any of this then take an hour to sit quietly in the corridor or day lounge of a home for the elderly and ask them whether having a visitor is important. Ask them if they care about whether their visitor brings a gift or how they feel about knowing that someone cares enough to remember them. To them what matters is simply that someone has taken the time and energy to make contact and to get in touch. The presents mean far less than the contact, and the contact is a reinforcement that someone cares enough to be thinking of them.

So many people, so little time

You only have twenty-four hours in a day so you won't be able to fit in all the things you want to. Likewise you will struggle to spend time with everyone equally. Think hard about the value of some of the relationships you have relative to the amount of benefit you get from them and how you feel as a result of being around those people. Some will be friends, others relatives or work contacts.

Try to be a little more selective about how you give out the time in your calendar if you are only going to be more worn down as a result of having done so. As the phrase *"less is more"* is applied to mean that a bit of quality is better than a lot of mediocre items, I often think that the same thought can be applied to your own appointment diary.

Let your mobile go to voicemail now and again. After all, the reason you have that facility is so you don't have to answer the phone yourself every time! Let people know that you have time out for yourself now and again, or that you are with your family and will not be taking calls, or that you are visiting some friends and will get back to them when it suits you to do so.

Put your family first and ensure that there is some regular time each week when you get together and create something special.

I recall how, as a child, my parents always took me to the cinema on a Saturday morning or we would often go out early on a Sunday morning to walk in the country park or along the riverbank. The memories of those film shows and my familiarity with the footpaths and lanes that I still visit regularly in my adult life have their roots in those familiar traditions which were deliberately created by my parents.

What habits and traditions were important to you as a child, as a teenager and as a young adult?

The chances are that the feeling of belonging or of having an adult be interested in your well-being is just as important to your own children. Take time to give the same to yours.

We all appreciate when someone clears their schedule to give us their time and attention. If this is true from our own perspective, what must it be like for us to give that time and attention to someone else who needs it?

Stick with your commitments

If you say you will be home for hockey practice, or dinner, or a trip to the cinema, don't then ring home to say you have been delayed or that you have to work late. I know this from experience and it has cost me dearly! It might have been okay if it was an excuse a few times, but to be repeated week after week will get you in deep trouble and understandably so as you begin to realize that others may end up expecting you to let them down.

One of my friends keeps a special place in his diary for his commitments and I have been so impressed by this since discovering it. These are distinct from his appointments, which are normally times when he has to show up and be in meetings or with family. William's commitments are different. He will list the thing he has agreed to do and the date he has promised it by, as well as the outcome of achieving the commitment.

Next to these he has the penalty written down for not accomplishing the commitment. He actually writes down on paper the true cost of letting someone down if he does not deliver, fails to turn up, gets the report in late or misses the party.

In the sense of using this approach like an emotional bank account, he knows whether he is in credit or if he is at risk of becoming overdrawn with his feelings. Is this a little extreme? If it works for you to do something like this yourself then it does not matter what others might think about it.

Try it and see if the test produces fruit, namely that you break fewer commitments and honor more promises than you did before. If you can see progress in this approach as opposed to whatever method or behavior you were following before, then you know for yourself you are on track.

A promise to be there for someone is still a promise however you look at it. No matter that your train was late or that you needed to stop for gas and got delayed. In the eyes of the other person, maybe you should just have been on the earlier train or filled up with gas the night before.

I can't hold my hand up and say I don't understand this, as I have been late more times than I care to remember. It was only when I focused on the actual promise made that I found myself turning up on time or leaving early for my destination that I saw the excitement in the eyes of another when I arrived in a timely fashion and was there when I said I would be.

Your own peace of mind will be enhanced and those around you will notice and comment with pleasure on the change in your behavior.

Leave a learning legacy for your children

You created these wonderful little people. They came into the world because of you. Take the time to consider the many wonderful things you can do to make their life a little better for having been here.

I don't care whether you are still with their other parent, or what happened between the two of you along the way. In fact, I get riled when I hear people say that a single parent, regardless of whether they are raising the child or not, is of less value than two parents who raise their children together. You created a child and you have a responsibility, no matter the distance that may exist between you today. Try to communicate with one another.

Leaving a legacy does not mean something that they only consider or discover after you have gone, although that in and of itself could be a nice thing for them. Instead, I mean that your child would one day feel they know you better if you can tell them what it was like for you when you were a kid, that they could derive confidence and knowledge from understanding how you got through the tough times, which ones made you want to give up and how you overcame the challenges that allowed you to become who you are today.

- *Does your child know what it was like for you to grow up in the street where you lived?*
- *Do they have any idea about the crush you had in the second year at school, or the way your class teacher would make funny jokes and crazy stories up on the school bus when you went to the swimming pool with your whole class?*
- *Have they ever heard the songs that your own parents would sing you to sleep with at night, or seen the words to those songs written down for them?*
- *What about the plays you were in at school, or the friends you had in the youth club, or the choir or the community walking holiday or the summer camp?*
- *Can you remember that time when you learned that the world was not just the place where you lived, and that there was even more out there than you had ever dreamed possible?*
- *How about the time that your grandparents showed you some piece of their own history, and you sat and listened to them telling you about how you were a part of that history yourself? It could have been a photograph, a map, a medal, a uniform, a program from a play that they were in or a playground game they had enjoyed as a child.*

Take the time to write this down and share with your own children because one day they may well want to have a sense of belonging to the family and need to tell the story to their own children.

I had long-remembered a time in the countryside with my Dad, my Grandad Tom and my Great-grandpa Charlie. For years it was a sort of imagined color picture in my mind until I was in my forties and my own father gave me a photograph of that day from when I was just two years old. I was in the cottage garden of my Great-grandpa Charlie. He was there bent over a spade, planting flowers in the company of his son, grandson and me as his great grandson This made it seem more real and more special than ever before. It also showed me that my memory of those happy times had been right.

Just writing about that discovery brings tears to my eyes again today, but do you know what? The fact that the picture existed and my Dad gave it to me in a digital scrapbook of family pictures meant so much to me. I have shared these images with my own boys, explaining to them who was who in each picture and hoping they may one day be motivated or interested enough to do the same.

So get on with it soon. Put that scrapbook together for them to have something special to hold onto, to look back at and know where they came from. Include in it some pictures you drew as a kid yourself, a photograph, a few pages from an old school report, some stories about your parents and the places you have lived, a diary extract, a letter from a relative, or a joke from an old school magazine.

Leave them with something that reveals more of you and allows them to know what a wonderful human being they came from.

Take a chance and spend some time simply being

yourself with them. Allow them the chance to see the open, friendly, loving and caring person inside you and they might just remember that moment for the rest of their lives.

And always, no matter how far you may be from them, remember their birthdays, for the day they came into the world was then and always will be truly special.

Just like them.

5

YOUR WORK

Do something you love

Many of us get locked into a routine of travelling to and from work in order to do something we dislike or even despise. We buy ourselves travel tickets or pick up transport costs in order to get to this place, where we are often surrounded by people we care little for and produce output we may have no connection with or little pride in. There is so much more to life than this.

You know that you have talents. It is just that you are often the very last person on the planet who will acknowledge this to be true. Hobbies, intellectual skills, passionate interests, technical curiosity or just a willingness to learn something new: it does not matter what the skill set or special ability is, so much as you being willing to spot it and acknowledge it for what it is - the seed of a new potential.

Consider that there are people making a living from

every single possible profession and occupation, and many of them do very well. If in doubt, pick up a commercial phone directory or look at a Local Pages website showing you the businesses in your own area. From Antiques to Zoology, people are making a good living or a decent income for themselves in activities they enjoy.

Through the expression of ourselves in our work, we also find connection to others. Maybe you achieve this through your job networks, or perhaps through the people you meet via your workplace and the associations you can make indirectly.

And many of them don't go to a distant work place in order to be successful. Tens of thousands of people within a short distance from you work from home doing something that pays its way. This may be via email, a web page, a mail-order operation, brokering deals by telephone, or liaising between people wanting their skills. It does not matter what they do, so much as that they do that thing which they are motivated by and drawn to.

Identify your own skills and passions and look to create revenue for yourself that you can build from home, or that you can sell with confidence to a prospective employer who would rather have enthusiastic and motivated people on their staff.

In encouraging you to explore the enjoyment of your work, I also want you to get closer to that place of attaining financial freedom. This is the freedom that you have when you never omit doing something for lack of money and that you never do anything that you don't want simply to get the money that is being offered.

If I put this another way, financial freedom is putting money to work for you instead of you having to work for money.

In order to make your own financial success, it will help you greatly to build yourself a prosperity mindset. This means that you can operate successfully and easily in the material world whether you have money or not. This is what a Prosperity Consciousness does for you.

A simple exercise to identifying work that can be enjoyable and which can sometimes lead to a new self-employed career was shared with me by my friend and mentor, Jim Leonard. You simply take a piece of paper and a pen and spend a few minutes writing down your ten favorite pleasures.

This is the simplest of exercises and yet it can be of enormous value to you in terms of both fun and money!

First, write down the ten things you most enjoy doing.

Next, have a look at these ten activities and underline the one which you enjoy most of all - and the one which you are the most willing to receive money for doing!

Now, looking at that same list and at the activity you have chosen from among the ten, work out how you can provide a service with that activity. Write down ten ways in which you can receive money from providing this service.

Choose one that you enjoy and have a go at it for a few weeks. Once you have developed money from the idea, move onto another manifestation of money with a different idea or service. You will then find it is very easy to produce money when you want it. Once you can produce money at a sufficient rate for your needs, you will begin to develop the ability to create funds flowing in while you are asleep, or when money is the last thing on your mind.

Putting time and focus into developing and creating *meaningful* work is one of the highest callings you can follow.

Make it second best to family and home

Work is a good thing, and it can be a great thing if it is something you love, but don't let it be the number one thing. There is so much more that is of value, gives joy and brings you deep satisfaction. Besides, you can always go back to work another day if you want to!

While it is true that your work can make it possible for you to find the money and the opportunities to be with those who mean so much to you, it is not the same thing as actually being with them. Work in and of itself is simply a way for you to spend your time, raising invoices perhaps if you are self-employed or pulling down a salary each month. There are obviously rewards and fees to be had from your work, but at what blend of results versus family or emotional losses?

Don't make your private life come second to a cold desk or a hard-nosed filing cabinet or that "damned meeting" or whatever other name the excuse takes. There is no need to avoid the important long-term values in your life for something that this time next month you will not be able to remember or put a name to.

Get your priorities right and ensure that work is not at the top of them. You will always have a chance to catch up on your work. For years I mistakenly thought that if I did not get a piece of work done and emailed out, or a property sold on a certain day, that my day would have been wasted or my life less worthwhile. How wrong I was, but it took me several critical problems in my own life to see how unrealistic I was being.

You can never catch up on a missed birthday, a wedding, a graduation, or an anniversary that you forgot because you have been distracted.

Where work is a true passion and an outlet for your spirit and your emotion then ignore some of what I have just said! If the emotional pull of what you have designed your working life around is creating such mental and heart-felt satisfaction for you, then I know you have to follow it. What counts is that you can apply yourself to the passion of your work with results that can be measured and not just as time spent without result. It is a difficult balancing act between work that is a passion and relationships that also mean the world to you, but you will be able to do it given the right support and encouragement.

First, get a hold of your own priorities in terms of work and expression and then get them right. Identify what these priorities are and determine to protect them.

Avoid the commute. Keep the focus and reward

Perhaps this is similar to suggesting that you control your own environment and asking you to focus on this within the context of work.

Within my own community there are many successful

people who own and run large businesses with staff either based locally or internationally, and others who have a few staff and work in the town.

A characteristic shared by many of these neighbors who are truly successful is that they rarely travel far from their businesses. Another way to interpret this might be to say that they avoid having the distractions of travel and having to respond or react to other people's timetables. Instead, they recognize the importance of maintaining a strategic focus on their work, staying close to the pure heart of what they excel at doing.

Take a close look at your own work routine. Of the time that you allocate to being either at or in work, how much of that is productive in the sense that it creates revenue and other measurable benefit for you?

If, as an example, you could determine that perhaps one third of your working time is what yields the results, how much more might you create if you successfully expanded this block of time and received a corresponding increase in results? Or only worked that amount of time and allocated the rest to leisure and relaxation?

The opportunity to spend a better proportion of your time in the activities that bring you rewards is not best served through wasting time in traveling, being away from your own workplace or getting involved in roles that could be better delegated and left to others.

When a successful friend of mine was asked by a start-up business owner why he no longer did some of the basic jobs, his reply was both very simple and most illuminating:

"Why", he said, *"would I want to do anything that only pays me $10 or $50 an hour if I can pick up a phone and dial out for someone else to do it? That leaves me free to create ideas and products where my involvement and leadership is worth 10 or 20 times that."*

Are you doing what works and what matters? Are you engaged in Meaningful Work? Can you let go of some of the stuff that comes across your desk and give it away, keeping your focus on what gets the best results for your own investment of time and attention?

See it as service

Once you can recognize that the work you do is a service to others, that they have a need for what you offer, then the process of work becomes something else, something special. It is as if you can see in your own offering the solution that others have been searching for. Take the time to look at what you do and at the skills you have as something that people have been waiting for.

So many people I speak with express the frustration they feel in their jobs, unacknowledged, less involved than they wish, and with heartfelt views and opinions that are rarely consulted. The pain and distance from true fulfilment that we can all identify with so strongly is the opposite of the opportunity for involvement and the recognition we yearn for. Being able to deliver a role that is appreciated and recognized is a true driver we can identify with and connect to strongly. Through such links with emotionally nurturing work and finding personal expression through our work we can achieve immense satisfaction.

In the way you go about your daily tasks, see how the sense of taking care of others is represented. In delivering your service, others directly benefit. Perhaps this is because you simplify a process for them so they do not have to keep struggling with it. Maybe you bring clarity to a problem that has long been troubling them. Then again, it could be that you are just good at what you do best. Whichever it is, others will line up to pay you for this skill.

Whatever angle you approach your work from, see the gains that your abilities bring to your client group and continue to do whatever is necessary to ensure that others benefit from you working with them or on the matters that help them.

Whether they are internal clients and colleagues from within your organization, or external customers, we all interact with people each day and the scope to do so from a place of service gives you focus for your work that will bring deep satisfaction.

Explore what skills you have and which you have yet to develop that can bring you the benefit of a deep sense of personal fulfilment from your work. If you are to spend years engaged in activities for which you get paid, then at least make sure that this work is something that brings a variety of rewards to you. The need for personal satisfaction is one of the most heartfelt desires we have and the scope to satisfy this demand through your work is so important.

Identify what others will see as a solution to their

needs and maintain your focus on providing your skill set to meet those needs.

Be a mentor to one other person

My friend Ray Harris of New Orleans often spoke with me about the importance of role models when he was growing up. At different times in these critical years, people appeared in his life at just the time that he required help and support. When he was in school a particular teacher took Ray under his wing and introduced him to the joy of reading and the magic of words. Slowly but surely Ray saw his ability with words grow to match his hunger for the books that were placed in front of him.

When he left school and was getting work experience, the right employer turned up at the right moment to give him an insight into what an experience of benevolent and caring employment should look and feel like.

As he entered the world of work and adult responsibility yet another man came forward to provide Ray with a model of decent, ethical behavior, and of a value system he could adopt with confidence.

Life is difficult and confusing enough as it is. If there is scope for lifting the load for someone you work with or cross paths with - and you are willing to do so - then pick up the gauntlet and rise to the challenge. Offer a hand up (as opposed to the charitable hand out) to an individual who strikes you as able to benefit from or appreciate the additional input you can give.

Ray has always taken the view that he was blessed with the support he received from outside his family and this led him into an active participation in "Each One Help One", an organization dedicated to matching mentors with those requiring that little bit of extra help.

Regardless of your age, experiences, work history or appetite for life, there is someone out there who is absolutely ready for the input, guidance and contribution you can provide.

Make yourself available and you will make a huge difference. Until you make the first step toward a mentoring organization, they will not know that you are there with the requisite strengths that are needed by someone they represent.

Think win-win

If life is viewed as a conflict through which you struggle, then for each win that can be attained, someone else has to lose and give up their own claim for a position or a result.

Rather than see and experience the ups and downs of that approach, consider instead the great pleasure that comes from a deal or a transaction where both you and the other person can each benefit from the activity.

You both win. You each see a positive outcome that you can be satisfied about and are happy with. The gain is a mutual one that you can each see something to be grateful for. This is a far cry from the historic and too often perpetuated lose-win or win-lose.

This win-win perspective may not be one that all people have, but what matters is that you choose it now for yourself. You can contribute to another person while still getting the outcome you desire for yourself and for your business or situation.

What would the alternative be? More struggle, more competition and more cause for concern over an outcome where someone is always trying to gain the upper hand. Why go back there?

Within one of my own businesses there were several years where we endured a financial roller coaster that eventually led to my own bankruptcy. This came about in part as a result of thinking that we had to win. Of course, there were always other players, other contenders for the rewards. I had been naive not to grasp this point earlier. However, the humility that such loss can bring with it is a good lesson and I switched to a different business model where I simply agreed with whoever brought me new business that we would split the fees equally. It was an act of faith and a new way of thinking but has meant financial recovery could proceed, and has also brought me closer to my business partners and colleagues for we now each benefit from the shift in focus. If we help one another to succeed, we each benefit.

In your next meeting, negotiation or committee session, look to see if the outcome of the event could take a different turn from the usual. Consider a possibility that instead of someone losing in order for you to win, there could be a new way where each party gains something of value to them.

It will not be the case that this is always feasible or possible. However, if you can now begin to see the possibilities for an outcome that reduces the need for others to lose in order for you to gain, then this is a result going forward.

If they don't like you, it's not personal

Having been a salesperson for years, I learned early on that if people don't buy from me there is another person waiting for my call. I used to have a terrible time in sales and life success until I realized this point.

In my first weeks out of university, knowing that I wanted to be around people and liked the principle of selling, I managed to get myself an interview with an office equipment company. I passed this and ended up being out on the road with my company car and sample machines. I felt physically ill sometimes trying to book appointments and then trying to sell a machine once I was there. However, once I could separate the fear of rejection from the process of selling, life and my work became a lot simpler.

One of the reasons it became simpler was that I realized that selling office products was not what I wanted to do, and I found other products and offerings I felt a better connection to. The other reason - and the one that was the most important in terms of feeling good about myself - is that I grasped the concept that it was a numbers game as well as being about relationships. By putting more effort into learning better skills with people, as well as stepping away from situations that were unprofessional, I began to enjoy the selling industry. I also started to get better results because I was focusing more on what the prospects wanted than on what I had done before, which was to make them want my product.

Often they were as keen to find someone to listen to them and to be able to hear the problems they were facing. If I had a solution for their issues, even better! Where there was simply no common ground between us, no mutual reason for being in contact with each other, then as soon as I let go of the need to feel liked or appreciated, the pain was gone. Either there was a working opportunity to do some thing or there was not, and no amount of being nice or wanting to be liked would make any difference at all.

This is true for life in that regardless of whether you are suggesting an opportunity, building a friendship, developing a network, or simply getting through your day, you are bound to be in contact with people you just cannot relate to. The fact that they feel the same is nothing to be concerned about.

Just find someone who either likes you and what you have to offer, or someone who just likes the offer because it is what they need and have been looking for. Either way you win. Both of you.

Get out of your own way

Time to be honest with yourself again. What do you know that you don't do well, do badly, or can't even do at all?

You can carry on the way you have been until now, getting stuck on your own failings, inadequacies and weaknesses, or you can choose to focus on the things you know you do well and either let go of or give away so many of the areas that are clearly not your strengths.

In your own journey there are so many things that you do with ease, brilliance, energy and sophistication. But you have to draw the line somewhere and acknowledge that there are some things where you hold yourself back, or even sabotage what could otherwise have been an enjoyable event or experience by choosing to think you can do better or know better.

Consider the possibility that you could simply stop doing some of the "stuff" that others could do better and in less time. Let go of the desire to think you have to be right all of the time. Allow yourself instead to be involved with the things and activities where you can make a valid and useful contribution.

For me it was letting go of trying to be in morning meetings and recognizing that my body clock just could not do it. The freedom and exhilaration I experienced when I stopped booking morning appointments was great, not just because it took the pressure off me, but because it also allowed me to stop disappointing clients by turning up late or not turning up at all!

For a colleague who lives locally, it was letting someone else deal with their post and email management, giving up the struggle with adamantly believing that he had to do it all himself.

For a neighbor with a retail store it was the issue of constantly comparing herself against another similar business in the next town, and wasting time unproductively in worrying about whether her own customers might go over to the other business. Instead, she developed a focus on what was great about her own offerings and why clients should spend their time, energy and money in her business. The happier she was in her work environment the more obvious this was to her clients and they did more business with her.

What is it that you are trying to do, and what can you let go of?

6

YOUR RELATIONSHIPS

They don't grow on trees

But they do develop from seeds! From the seeds of a smile, a kind word, a listening ear, from an opportunity to be shared and from a moment in which a decision is made that brings you closer to someone. In much the same way that we will plant surplus seeds to bring in the anticipated harvest, so too we can sow the seeds of a relationship by simply giving generously to that relationship.

Leaving aside the natural harvest analogy, recognize that any relationship is developed. They do not just happen. If they did, the interaction between two people would be called a meeting and not a relationship. And where a meeting can be a formal, structured and one-off event, by comparison a relationship is the place where so much more can happen.

Relationships at their best are supportive and nurturing. They can bring fulfilment and deep satisfaction. However, working and delivering these benefits requires an interaction of energies and a blending of intention. As you look about the map of connections and engagements that you have with those around you, there will be no escaping your awareness of what constitutes a good relationship and what distinguishes this from those of lesser depth and quality.

Take a look at the relationships you have and listen to what your own intuitive sense tells you about those that bring benefit, richness, support, caring and nourishment, and those that drain the life force out of you, or which are simply neutral in terms of bringing in less than you put into them.

Invest time in cultivating the relationships that surround you. Where a good connection looks to be lost then consider what might be done to first protect and strengthen it, before you face its loss. When you feel a bond with someone, do all that you can to encourage its growth.

You do this because you know in your heart that the human condition is about relationships at its core. About the links - invisible or otherwise - that bind us to other people, showing us the similarities that we so love to observe and move toward.

You have to work at them

My wise friend Bob Mandel once said to me that *"Love is not a noun, but a verb, a doing thing that requires effort and energy."* Namely, you have to put work into love to make it happen. Relationships are part of the same process.

If a relationship is to continue after it starts or to

develop from a given point, it has to be seen as something flexible, malleable, and ever-changing. The relationship you have with one person is as much subject to your input as to the input and exchange they get from the rest of their network and peer group. However, you can only be responsible for the contribution that you make yourself.

Building support and enhancing people skills is work in the true sense of the word. But in a natural relationship, where there is a point of connection, the effort or the "work" is not of the same type. It requires instead that you actively take part, that you bring yourself and your focus to the place of two people coming together.

There will be times in any relationship where you need more from it than you are contributing yourself and then the situation will change and you will become more of a giver, bringing strength to the arrangement. Simply being aware of this ebb and flow will allow you to have a sense of perspective and to be realistic about the exchange of energy that you observe to be needed. To stop giving and end the contribution will see you losing the relationship, or at least no longer receiving so much from it.

Place your energy and your intention into the creation of a relationship that gives each of you a healthy sense of being welcome, having something to contribute, of being in a space where judgment is absent.

Your input and commitment to the relationship can bring satisfaction beyond measure, as you build upward from a foundation of understanding, appreciation and love. Your own input, sharing, supporting and encouraging can bring you all you will ever need.

Do the 'work' and receive the reward of relationships that are both fulfilling and giving.

Don't take people for granted

Easier said than done perhaps. However, you know what it feels like to be taken advantage of or - at the other end of the emotional spectrum - to be loved unconditionally. There are very different outcomes from what could potentially be the same starting point.

Consider the relationships and friendships you have now and look at each one with a view to understanding whether you are giving as much to it as you are taking from it.

Is there someone who would be grateful if you invested yourself and your energies into that situation?

Would they be relieved if you took a greater share of the responsibility, or of the commitment, than you are at the moment?

And would contributing more yourself give you a different feeling about your role?

Have you made assumptions about what it might be that is important for you, but perhaps not appreciated or understood what these important requirements might be for the other person? We don't need to be nosy, pushy or intrusive in order to discover what the other person requires, or to learn what they might be going through privately. We can learn about their concerns and worries, their fears or doubts, by creating a place where they feel safe to share, and by also simply asking them *"What's the matter?"* or *"How can I help?"* or *"Can I do something for you?"*

In the same way that you don't want to feel put upon or taken for granted, consider the way that people will react and respond to such attention from yourself.

How might you better engage and connect with others in ways that are about the benefit, care and well-being of each of you, rather than just yourself?

Express thanks to your friend or to your colleague or business partner for the great things they do. Be clear with them that you truly appreciate what it is they bring to the relationship. Let them hear that you love the way they do something, or that their opinion and sharing of an idea or a suggestion really makes a positive difference and has value.

Do any or all of these things to show from your heart that you have an understanding of their gifts, and a gratitude for who they are and that you want them to know this.

Have relationships that support you

Supportive. Nurturing. Trusting. Inspiring. Loving. Encouraging. Affirming.

These are just a few words that might reflect some of the better relationships you have, yet they are very different from the words you might use to describe those relationships that are leading you in a different direction or to no place at all.

Leaving and letting go of relationships that are hurtful, abusive, painful and which contribute nothing to you is a far more difficult process than we might first imagine. Why would we allow ourselves to do anything that is hurtful to us, or allow anyone else to impose these negatives? There is no short answer to this.

To even begin to acknowledge to yourself that you are in a relationship that is at least difficult and at worst threatening to your well-being is a brave first step. Without the recognition of the facts of what is going on around you, it is very difficult to then take any action that moves you away from what is not working for you in this moment.

Believing in yourself is a strong beginning. It may take time for you to make this true, especially if you have let yourself be walked on or stepped over, or you have given away your self-esteem in the process of loving someone. Considering yourself and your well-being as sufficiently important and precious is a significant step in the right direction.

Where you experience a good relationship of caring or of friendship, expand this by spending more time on it and by placing more focus on the good that is already there. This will allow for the expansion of that which is already present in your life to grow into more of the same.

In the observation of good friends, the noticing of kindness, the allowing of patience or courage or nurture, let yourself see the display of these qualities and bring them further into yourself and your own daily experience. The more you can encourage this to happen, the less space there is for negative actions and behaviors .

Begin to attract to you more of that which you desire to experience. Do this simply and calmly by requesting it to occur in your daily being. You will begin to see the changes as soon as you request what you want. So ask for this to be here now for you.

Let go of the ones that hurt you

Addiction to unproductive, non-supportive, and hostile relationships is easy to get used to. This is precisely because you did not get here overnight. You gradually slipped into allowing it to become this way.

We all have a desire to be loved, wanted and appreciated. Sometimes though, we get confused about what constitutes a good relationship as opposed to one in which we seem to have a role that is perhaps less clear cut.

Being stuck in old patterns of relating to people might mean you are always the giver and yet you don't seem to be appreciated or nurtured in return. Perhaps you are not even acknowledged for the good person you are. Could it be that you are being taken advantage of?

On the other hand, maybe it could be the case that you are the one in some of your relationships where you are taking someone for granted, and their own contribution to the relationship is going un-noticed or un-acknowledged by yourself.

A simple stock check or tally of your important relationships will allow you to see what is working and what is simply painful or wrong.

Be clear with yourself and with the other person that

what has been tolerated until now can no longer be allowed to go on. Instead, you are unable to stay engaged in such a relationship and you will have to remove yourself from it. If this is a relationship that is temporary or one that is occasioned through work, then it is easier to deal with perhaps than where the relationship is a very significant one and closer to home.

But the truth remains: you cannot do any good to yourself or for yourself if you remain in a place that is no good for you. This is not an easy decision to make, and you may want to seek professional counsel or the guidance of a friend who already knows you well in order that you can have an opportunity to talk through your thinking and through the implications of any of the decisions you might seek to make.

In any of these discussions, maintain your focus on the real goal of letting go of the relationships that are not in your own higher interest.

How about the relationship with yourself?

How are things with you? Feeling good about who you are and how you are in yourself? Yes? No? Maybe? Confused? Welcome to the human race my friend! So often you might catch yourself during the day being concerned about the things in your life that seem to be unresolved, which cause you stress or worry and which you will rightly want to give some time to. The issue is that while so much is not dealt with, it can indeed be difficult to even think of yourself, let alone to consider the relationship that you have with yourself.

Answer this question for yourself:

"Today I feel . . . ."

Fill in the gap with a stream of thoughts and allow yourself to notice the feelings as you experience them. You may find this a potentially uncomfortable exercise to begin with as it is very unlikely you have deliberately taken time for yourself before. This is okay and a totally natural response. In this quiet time, you will be able to listen to yourself and hear what you are carrying around with you all the time.

Allow yourself and your spirit the time to let these thoughts flow into the present. Listen to yourself without judgement and just accept what you hear your thoughts telling you. Let these ideas, thoughts, apologies, sadnesses, embarrassments, affirmations and statements of fact be felt just as they are. Let go of the need to filter or change them. Simply receive and accept them.

Knowing these thoughts now, give thanks that you are aware of them and consider the impact that such thoughts will have had on you for as long as you have been holding them. At the very core of your relationship with all the people you come into contact with is this relationship that you have with yourself. Whether you are loving, hateful, caring, doubting or kind to yourself, this fundamental relationship with yourself is carried out into the world with you.

Begin to explore the feelings and thoughts, the considerations and the emotions that come up for you in this quiet reflection time that you are engaging in today.

Do not judge what you see and hear in this conversation with yourself. Simply resolve to take the points you observe and make use of them in a gentle way. Move forward from this place and determine to strengthen the relationship with yourself from your new knowledge.

You are an amazing person simply by being here in this moment. That you are here at all is a miracle of biology, nature, survival, determination and of the power and expression of love.

On those days when you might allow yourself a down moment (and we all have times like that), just consider the miracle of you being here at all and it might allay a few of your own doubts, fears and concerns, and reveal them for the insecure moments they represent.

The relationship you have with yourself is the most important of all. If you do not have love and respect for yourself, how then do you find love and give respect for another? If you already have a personal source of internal motivation and self-respect, it becomes so much simpler for you to provide this to others. You do this through a sharing of a part of yourself, by revealing some aspect of who you are and what you stand for.

Of course, you get to that place through questioning yourself about who you are and who you have become so far in this journey we call life.

Be easy on yourself. Simply accept who you are and what you are here for. Perhaps not the simplest quest to find the answers to! There is a great opportunity here for you and the act of having a good relationship with yourself can come from starting with your focus on a good relationship. You can improve the whole thing and move onwards and upwards from there!

Above all, be a source of your own love.

7

YOUR WELL-BEING

Stress, worry and fear - acknowledge it

Too much to do and too little time in which to do it? Too few resources with which to achieve it. Maybe even both!

If you are anxious about travelling to work, worried about your performance when you are there, distracted by worry from being present with your family and loved ones, then face the stress head on and be honest that you have it. It could be your workload, financial pressure, relationship dissatisfaction, or health matters. Any number of things have the potential to place you under pressure that is difficult or even impossible to cope with.

You may feel tension in your mind or body. It could be that you are experiencing pressure on your ability to lead a life that is satisfying. Being aware of the stress and being honest enough with yourself that it is there is the first important step, and then you can begin to take action to deal with it one piece at a time.

The other aspect of looking at stress is noting how it

is affecting your wider life. I know that when I face more stress I become irritable and poor company, and I can be grumpy and short tempered. More positively than this though, I know that if I let others know the pressure I am feeling and the way it is impacting me then they can understand why I act that way. Once they are aware of this then they are free to help me, to participate in my own recovery from the downward spiral or simply know to let me be and to allow me the space to start working through it!

Until you are honest with yourself about the issues you face, you will find neither the time, resources or energy to deal with it and your situation will simply deteriorate. Take action now before the problem becomes more serious and requires further external help and support.

Worry is a strange thing, part defense mechanism, part self-protection. An ancient defense mechanism, in its best format it exists to keep us alert and to encourage us to stay sharp in case of danger that we think is lurking somewhere out in front of us. Yet too much worry, too great a focus on worry and that same behavior has converted itself into looking for trouble when it is not there, into dark imaginings that will render you permanently fearful and ever dreading that the worst is about to happen.

We both know that statistics, logic and probability mean that what you are worrying about is unlikely to come to pass, but in the act of worrying you don't help yourself at all. It is very much the case that what your mind focuses on is further enabled and given more presence.

For example, if you worry about meeting and paying your household bills on time, you can get yourself into such a state of concern that you will magnify the problem and begin to draw more bills to you in the process! You are an attractor and you draw to you the same energies that you send out into the Universe. With this example of bills, you can reduce your worry by agreeing to spend only a certain amount of your time thinking about the bills. Beyond this, imagine and visualize instead the bills being paid on time and in full. Visualize the *PAID WITH THANKS* stamp upon each of your bills. See the post arriving at your house each day, perhaps with a check in the mail, or with online credits to your bank account. See refunds being issued to you. Do this instead of multiplying the worry factor.

Sure, this is a cute example and does nothing to allay your fear about the things that concern and worry you. But please help yourself by thinking about the external influences on your thinking and which may well be placing their own seeds of fear and doubt in your mind. The television and the radio news don't focus on providing you with positive and inspiring stories. Instead they report on negative actions that serve only to create more fear in your mind. As an experiment, let yourself do a day without either watching or listening to the news. You'll survive the day, and after a week of this you will also begin to see a reduction in the thoughts and fears that have been affecting your well-being for the worse.

Fear can be crippling in the way it affects your

thinking and begins to push its way into your conscious and unconscious thoughts. The fear of the unknown is one aspect that can be dealt with in a logical way, i.e. if it is unknown then there is an element of being able to contain and explain the fear.

However, where a fearful imagination exaggerates existing challenges or troubles and making them many times worse, this can be crippling to those experiencing the fear as well to the people around them.

The exaggeration of small concerns or fears can be such that one person in the relationship can see the distortion that fearful person can no longer perceive. When this happens it can be very challenging for the observer to stay within the context of the conversation or discussion before the whole situation grows out of proportion.

Seeing only from a perspective of logic is not always helpful to the person experiencing fear either! Many times I have heard from clients where one person is in the grip of a fear that they cannot truly explain to their more logical partner. Sometimes the best solution is not for an answer to be found at all, but for the person with fear to simply be heard; allow them to share what is hurting them and causing them such anguish. You can actually talk your fears out.

As human beings there is an ancient survival need for us to experience elements of stress, worry and fear. How else would we have survived attacks from saber-toothed tigers and cave bears thousands of years ago if it had not been for these emotions giving us the 'fight or flight' response to imminent danger? But the tigers and the bears have been replaced by utility bills and corporate takeovers that threaten potential redundancy; by the mountain of email where each sender expects we will respond to them immediately; by pressures at work; and by society to conform to the expectations that co-workers and neighbors have of us. No wonder we can fall victim to stress as we go through our own daily lives.

But, and this is a big but, there is no need for us to let the three demons of stress, worry and fear intimidate us and force us to lower our heads in submission. Life is filled with great opportunities, and with tremendous scope for joy and satisfaction. Yet it seems that the more automated, structured and digital our lives become, the easier it is to be overwhelmed by the amount of data traffic, conversations, work transactions, social media posts and information we imagine we need to manage and handle. As a result, it is hardly surprising we feel scared, concerned and anxious that we will be unable to cope.

Acknowledge what you can and cannot tolerate as acceptable levels of stress and worry, and begin to eliminate the causes of those, to reduce the impact of the various pressures and to work out corrective changes to what you are going through in order to reduce the stress you are presented with.

Life is not easy when you are facing such pressures, but it is important for you to consider *what is* and *what is not* acceptable in terms of the causes. Where possible, take action to correct what is not working and to see what is out of context with your own value system. So often the issues can be diminished by seeing how they are out of sync with what matters to you in the first place, and adjusting from there.

Make time for yourself

Letting life get on top of you to the extent that you are both physically and emotionally dragged down by it is the beginning of a slippery slope. There are no hard and fast rules as each of us is different. However, it is easy to find yourself living for other people, for someone else's priorities or diary schedule, leaving very little for yourself. You get physically spent and come home at the end of each day wiped out, exhausted, unable to make a move other than perhaps grab a drink and a TV remote control.

Time is just as much a resource as money, and yet we still often struggle with the concept of paying ourselves first. Let me explain. When your income comes in each week or each month, if you will first take 10% of the gross amount and pay it into a savings account before allowing the rest to be spent on the day-to-day bills, you know with total certainty that you will have a one month equivalent income set aside in just ten months, two months in twenty months, etc.

You can recognize the sense of making an investment in your future finances starting now. With this being the case, it is surely a simpler thing to invest in your own well-being, and to look at your own energy levels and see whether they are up and going up higher, or down and falling. But if I ask you to take your calendar and look at the commitments you have given to other people, what have you got in there for yourself? Have you given so much away that you have little time in there for yourself.

You need to stake a claim for yourself and be in the place that allows you to nurture yourself and see your own growth. This is what I mean by putting yourself first in your diary.

At the start of this coming week, mark out the diary time you want to set aside for yourself and your values. Do this for the hobbies and activities you want to get on with, but which you have been procrastinating over. There is no one else out there who will value your own time as much as you, so you have to seize the moment for yourself. Do not allow someone else to dictate your diary after work hours.

If your work hours are not productive for you, or if the schedule you work is proving to be counter-productive to leading a life of success and happiness, then you have some planning to do and a decision to make about what it is that you truly want your life to look like.

When someone wants you to give them an hour of your life and asks that you give away this time for free, be clear with yourself that time given to such a meeting has value and is either in alignment with your own intended success or is instead an unproductive distraction. Where that person requests an appointment and you have no wish to give your time away, say so. Feel confident about simply saying *"I already have a prior engagement"* without feeling the need to say what else you are doing.

Start this week and make a planning appointment with yourself. Could you put thirty minutes each day in your diary that is just for you? What about sitting down and blocking out one day each month that is your day? You could binge watch a series, go out with friends, take part in a class, walk by the river or take a ride on your bike. The point here is to give yourself some time for you.

This could well be the beginning of a wonderful new phase in your life where you start to see and to experience that you are really free to choose to do those things that you love and enjoy. You will find doors opening to you and new people coming into your life with every wish for your best.

Enough is enough!

When your heart is pounding with fear and your own sense of well-being is shot through with concerns, worries and disappointments, or you find yourself grinding to a physical and mental halt, you have to call a time-out. To say aloud *"Enough is enough!"* and really mean it.

If you are not there for yourself, then who else are you truly able to be there for?

You have to stop doing what is no longer working for you. Say "No" to those activities or actions that drain and exhaust you. Stop associating with the people who - just by you being in their company - draw the life force from you. If this sounds drastic, please face the alternative - allowing things to get worse with your permission and agreement!

Think about those activities, social gatherings and relationships that literally 'take it out' of you. The 'it' is the energy, vibrancy, color, warmth and personality that is the true you. If you engage in activities that affect you less than positively, you need to rethink your involvement in them.

And guess what? As you withdraw from such non-beneficial or even destructive things, you will feel stronger, enjoy more time for you, re-charge your life battery and see your circumstances reframed anew.

The more you do this for yourself, the sooner you will see a shift in what happens around you. Call a halt to the activities, interruptions, time wasters and resource drainers that serve you not at all. Strike them from your schedule wherever possible, and replace them with time for yourself, for your passions, and your own sense of living your life on purpose. Remember that this is all about Simple Self Help.

Listen to your own inner mind, to the wisdom that is always close at hand for you. Ask your inner guide for assistance in finding the access to what is right for you. In a place of calm within you, step to the sounds and colors that attract you, nourishing you in this time of quiet.

This is your life. You can hold the reins and step towards your own significance. No need to apologize, to explain unless you want to, or to feel that you should give up any more of who you are. Make today your day and only allow into it those people and activities that lift and strengthen you.

Stop chasing rainbows

In a book such as this where I want to encourage you to pursue your dreams, achieve your goals and do what is right and good for you, this might seem a strange heading to begin with. But the rainbows I want you to avoid are the ones that promise everything and give you nothing. They are the false hopes, the glittering shadows, the mirages that disappear as you walk toward them.

You have all you need to live a fulfilling life, but you might have forgotten this truth. It might be that you have the food you need, or the love, or the space to be yourself, or perhaps the opportunity to be creative, to express yourself. You know the truth of this right now.

There are so many attractive toys and trinkets and must-have items out there. Of course there are! But do you need them to make your life more complete in this very moment? I doubt it. Yes, they might make tomorrow look nicer and better, but you don't live in tomorrow, you have today.

Both in business and personal circles we see the time wasted by people chasing after the trophy goals and the prize items only to discover either that they feel no different when they reach them. Even worse, they acknowledge what they may have lost in a personal or human sense by the relentless pursuit of the empty goal.

Get on with your life as it is right now. Consider the things that are important to you and the way you seek to live and to lead your own life. Take comfort from the fact that others have been this way before you, and that there is help at hand as you make your own way along the route that is right for you.

Look at the good friendships you do have, at the person who cares about you, at the people who respect you for something you have done or for a goal realized.

Notice the achievements you had yesterday and the pleasure you felt at a kind act you did. Be aware of the gratitude that you received recently from someone for a simple gesture you made towards them.

All of these and more are true, reminding you of all the good that you already have and are able to receive now and always. Of course there are more great experiences and good things to be had, people to meet and connect with, and all of this will happen normally and within a timetable that will make itself known when the timing is right. Simply allow life to give you all the gifts it has for you and which you can accept in the moment. You don't need to push or chase.

Be grateful

One of the least understood miracles of this amazing life is that you attract what you place your focus on. So if you have complaints about how bad things are for you, instead of seeing things improve you will notice more and more of the unpleasant stuff pile up outside your door, waiting to come in. It can feel like nothing is ever going to get better, as if your world is going to collapse.

In my own experience, there have been several times when I was stuck in a problem and continued to make the situation worse. At such times the debts were piling up and the creditors were getting angrier. I made things worse by panicking and by throwing myself into a pitiful state of mind, imagining things getting increasingly bad. The days were so painful that it seemed that all I could do was work endless hours and yet I made no progress at all. Such difficult times, when they ended, came about because of a shift in my thinking, in the way I was using language and more than anything else because I stopped complaining and began to express my gratitude. Gratitude for what the experience was teaching me, for the opportunity I was receiving to learn about new skills, for the good things I could acknowledge and for the money that I did actually have. In this way the troubles diminished, new work showed up for me and I began to notice opportunities which had been right in front of me all that time. I could not see them until I adjusted my attitude and my perspective.

By shifting your focus onto the good things, people and lessons you do have, you begin to let go of the hassles, and start to receive more beneficial happenings and a greater flow of abundance, love and energy.

Gratitude for what you do have can bring about profound change. Start with where you are now.

Today, for example, I am writing at home with beautiful weather outside. Sheep are in the fields surrounding the house. I have a lovely blue sky and a gorgeous landscape beyond the windows. I am enjoying a great cup of coffee and writing with a beautiful pen that flows across the paper. My children are enjoying time on the beach. I am doing what I love and in this moment all is well. I am very grateful for all of this right now.

How about you? In this moment what can you be grateful for? What can you think about that you can express your gratitude and thanks for? Look at the things that you can appreciate.

Remember that what you focus on will expand and

bring you more of the same. If you would like to receive more of what you want, take the time to give thanks for what you have already and trust that the Universe wants to provide you with more. Let it happen. Allow it to happen.

8

YOUR LOVE

Give it

You never know when you cross paths with someone else quite how much, in that instant, they need to feel your love. You may wander around thinking that your own life could be better, about how nice it would be to get a break now and then, or what if it just worked out right for yours truly, but think about the needs of someone else.

Today, tonight, tomorrow morning, or next month. It scarcely matters. Someone is out there crying in pain or desperately in need of some love. Maybe they just need some belief, some encouragement and some contact. You might just well be the person to provide it for them right there and right now. In a wonderful twist of irony, the more you give love, the more you will receive love yourself. But that need not be a motivation for you to give and to share your love.

When an opportunity comes around, take it, live

through the moment and give what you know you should.

Don't hold back, either for fear of being no good or for doubt that what you have may not be enough. Give of yourself and do not judge the process. Be free in the moment to allow yourself to release the good you have and the good that you are.

Life will ask you to share your love sometimes when it might seem unclear to you why. At other times, life will place you in a moment where it is obvious that you are there either to give or to receive love and you will simply know what is to be done.

The excellent and thought provoking 'Course in Miracles' book makes the beautiful statement that *"...there only two emotions: Love and Fear."*

With this being so, then by giving love you create a place where what you give is magnified and the love you choose to focus on will come back to you multiplied.

The same is equally true of fear. But to spend more time in a state of fear and to receive the magnification of that same fear decreases the scope and the opportunity for you to receive love and its associated benefits. When you sense fear, share your love. Each time you notice fear in yourself, switch to noticing the feeling and the sensation of love and you will see the fear subside.

There is no limit to love, or a cup of it that does not overrun when needed. Love is always present and around you, ever seeking you, ever available to you. Understand this to be so.

In the moment that you choose love, it creates not only more love for you, but also opens doors that no amount of logical words or persuasive argument would ever have scope of undoing.

Focus on love and share it with total confidence that love is always both the highest option and the only real way to be in any given moment or situation.

Forgiveness: yourself and others

So many people walk around with their heads down and their hearts heavy as they go through life. Either they feel that life has been bad to them, or they know that they have been hurt by someone else or by a circumstance. They cannot bring themselves to let go of these negative feelings inside.

To carry around a feeling of hatred or a desire to get even with someone will only hasten your own demise and cause untold physical as well as emotional damage. Each day that passes with you harboring ill-feeling towards someone only hurts you. Why? Because the other person might not even know or remember what they did that caused you to feel so much bad energy.

In the wonderful film '*The Shawshank Redemption*', a prison inmate says to his friend that they have a choice about the way they (and therefore you) respond to life and the challenges placed in front of you. He says, *"You either get busy living or you get busy dying."*

Take a quiet moment, or part of a quiet day, to be clear about the benefits you are receiving by hanging onto the pain and anger of not forgiving someone their behavior against you. You might even write them a note, explaining how you feel, how you have believed yourself to have been wronged, and that you wish to move on with your life now and be free to receive more joy and pleasure.

You don't need to actually send them the letter or note, and you probably don't even know where they live nowadays if you have been hanging on to this pain for a long time. You can put just their first name on it and actually mail it, knowing it can never be delivered. Or you could set fire to it with a candle and watch the letter turn to ashes on a plate, or even throw the letter in a fast-flowing river and watch it be carried away. Whichever way you choose to do it, and in whatever place you go through this simple yet powerful ritual, you are making a decision to let go and to forgive.

This process of forgiveness and letting go works just as well where you have done things you regret and still carry around the thoughts associated with that. Let go of the pain and get on with your life.

Let it all go ... Let it go now ... Release it ...

Forgive all the people who you once thought had wronged you or harmed you in some way.

Forgive those who you loved and where that love either died or turned into something less.

Forgive those from whom or around whom you have felt jealousy, shame, anger, fear and pain of any kind.

Do this regardless of whether it seems logically the right thing to do. Your heart is not logical. You are not even logical yourself. Simply understand that if you are holding on to some sense of having been wronged, hurt, mislead or deceived in the past, that just your thinking about this is reducing your ability and space to experience well-being, happiness and bliss right now.

No person and no experience that is from your past should have that hold over your enjoyment and your choice to have and to create your best life in this instant. Let it go. Let it go now. Just release it all.

Be present in the moment and realize all the good that you have and all the good that you are.

Forgiveness and letting go

There is a time, a moment, a feeling in which you know that you need to release your hold and let go. Sometimes we are saying goodbye and letting go of a situation that is no longer bearable even though we still love the person. It is just that we can no longer cope with our spirit being sapped and our radiance being extinguished by the other person. At other times, the letting go is forced upon us by a person who wants to leave us or by a bereavement.

Each of these scenarios is entirely different and there is no comparing the trauma of grief with the loss of a love who chooses to leave. Neither should we look too closely here at the reasons that a loving relationship ends. There is no pain quite so bitter as a love that has been twisted and lost. The hurt of a love that has been taken for granted and cast aside is equally deep.

Whatever the level of sadness, grief, discomfort or even anger, you need to get on with your own life, and to do this you must release and let go. Use the space created by the end of a relationship to contemplate and consider your next steps.

I once read a beautiful story about love and the way that, over time, we link ourselves in so many ways to the other person we love. Each trip out with them, every kiss, each cuddle, every time we chat or laugh or cry together, we make a connection between their soul and ours. It is as if a very strong and completely invisible string is created between us with each of these emotional interactions.

Over the time of the relationship the ties that bind us together are so many and so powerful that you literally cannot cut through them. This is not only because there are so many of these invisible cords, but also because each time you cut one of them, you are also cutting a part of yourself and cutting yourself is painful. At the end of a relationship the ties are still there, pulling on you even though the two of you are no longer together.

To dash headlong into a new relationship when the cords of an old one are still intact does not work for the very obvious reason that you are still tied to your former love. So spend time in ceremonies where you first loosen and then let go of the cords and create a space for your own being to be free again.

The process of these healing ceremonies can be held wherever you want, although nature is always a great place for them. You should include a time where you are saying *"Goodbye",* sending them a message of safe journey and God speed. If you did not release them, they would be forever in your presence, still exerting their influence on you.

Allow yourself the scope to step into a new space that is yours and within which you will be free to express who you are, acknowledge the relationship that was, to commence the process of healing and gather your own energies for the present moment.

See the process and the act of letting go as bringing closure to you, as a route to a different or even better point of your life here and now.

You can function well and be in a safe place even after the letting go and the release.

Let go and free yourself to regain who you are and to strengthen your spirit.

Attracting love

Love can find you unawares and sometimes at the very moment that you imagine it will never happen! Love is a wonderful tease when she wants to be and will make your heart race when you would expect it to be steady, or to leap when you thought it would simply stroll!

The best way to attract anything is actually just to be you, to do what pleasures, supports, strengthens and satisfies you. Too many opinions tell us that you should be a certain way, or follow a trend or a fashion. Since when was it right to be something and someone you are not? No. Stick with being the amazing, wonderful, special person that is you and see what you attract.

Look at what makes you the person you are. Consider the interests, the passions, the hobbies and the pastimes that give you joy and satisfaction.

Are you working in the role that is right for you and realizing the chance to share yourself with the world in a way that reflects your own skills and interests?

If someone who did not know you, and who had never met you, were to turn up at your home and look around your space, what would they see that reflects you living the life that is meant to be?

Would they discover a person who is engaged in fulfilling activity and spending their hours in activities that are truly them?

Or might they see a person whose attitude and mindset is: *"One day I'll do this or do that. Perhaps I might someday follow my heart and do what really motivates and thrills me. But not right now, maybe when the timing is right."*

Go through the rooms of your home and look at the clutter and junk that might be preventing more life from jumping in. How much unnecessary 'stuff' have you been hoarding and hanging on to in case it comes back into fashion or have a purpose? Spring clean your house, even if it is the middle of winter. Get rid of the things that bring neither function nor beauty of form into your living space.

You will draw to you people and experiences in harmony with the message that you are sending out from the core of your being. So it is with love. Your own attractor factor is the measure of the energy level about you. Work on enhancing your energy because that is what you want to do or because it simply feels right to do, and not for some exterior prompting or suggestion.

Don't wait for love to come calling. Instead, fill your days with activities that fulfill you and by being around people who make your spirit soar.

Love and spirited friendship will knock on your door

and ask to be let in because you are open to this delicious opportunity yourself.

Accepting and receiving love

Allowing love into your life is where so much of your happiness and fulfilment comes from. Not just romantic love, but platonic love, supporting love, and the gentle, caring love that finds expression in friendship.

For love to flourish it needs to be made welcome, to have a place set for it or for it to be able to arrive without notice and make its presence felt around you. Key to its arrival is the space for it to flourish and to be able to flow.

Be open to receiving, to accepting and embracing the arrival of love as well as the feelings and emotions that accompany it. If you fight against it, ask yourself why are you so reluctant to receive? If you close its point of arrival, what are you attempting to achieve in doing so?

Do you want to feel the warmth of love in your day, in your life? Then do those things necessary to allow it in, and stop doing those things which prevent it from being present.

So clear up the clutter that is blocking your life and causing so much personal and emotional stagnation. Put events in your calendar that bring you pleasure and enjoyment, as well as allowing you to get out and about and mixing with others of like persuasion.

Be open to the arrival of happiness, of joy and feelings of satisfaction and well-being.

To stop these would be to limit your own experience

of an abundant Universe and of a world that wants the best for you. Let the love in.

It will be remembered

The slipping of your hand into another. The soft laugh. A gentle embrace. And it is not just the touch, but just as strong is the feeling that you know you are loved. You know the love you can recall right now, even though the person who gave it to you, showered it on you, shared their love with you is no longer here.

And so the love will be remembered always as that most special of things that time and distance do little to reduce. How might it be that the love you share with someone today or tomorrow might resonate with them ten, twenty, thirty years from now?

It does not have to be earth shattering to be special, it simply has to be real and honest and openly shared and truly meant. This is plenty. Look at your own chances to express love with those you meet today or during the week that is ahead and remember - when you want to - to express your heart with those you choose to. It might be a special thank you or a meeting of the eyes, a touch on a shoulder, a warm embrace or a deep hug. All of these are important if freely given and naturally shared.

One evening I was talking with my youngest son as he got ready for bed. We were chatting about my Grandad Tom and how much he had loved me when I was a little boy. All of a sudden, in the middle of telling my own son about this time from my childhood, I felt myself over-whelmed by the love of my grandfather reaching out into the present to wrap me in his strong arms and remind me that I am still loved by him, that I am still his own little grandson so many years after he passed away. He was tangibly in the room with us for those minutes, being with his great-grandson through my sharing. Forty years from today that moment will still belong to my boy and the love will be remembered from a Great Grandpa he never knew but who he can glimpse through his father.

Love is a legacy in that it is not bound by time and space as so many physical things are. Love can be an act, a feeling, a metaphor, a message for someone you reach out to. It is best when not structured or controlled. It needs no boundaries imposed upon it, not will it respect measurement of it.

Do let your love show. Allow it the space to be of you and from you. It will make all the difference in the world to someone who receives it. You will be able to know that you did the right thing simply because you gave your love.

Look after the love you have

Neglect in relationships, just as in other precious matters, will see the tarnishing and then the loss of what you once cared so much about.

You don't only experience love as a feeling, you also need to work at it as an action.

All too often we have something special and we stop working at it in the way we did when that love first began. In the early days, we nurtured it like the seed of something that was growing into a stronger and more beautiful thing. We cared for it with attention and forethought, acts of kindness and intentional consideration. Unsurprisingly, it grew to become something special.

Special relationships like this can also become regular, steady and predictable. This does not happen intentionally on behalf of either party, but can happen with the demands of everyday life and experiences.

Building an ever deeper relationship, or simply maintaining the honor and specialness of a loving relationship, requires work, attention and energy, just like anything that is important to you. Just as you cannot expect to plant seeds in a field and wait idly for the harvest, so too is it not possible for you to expect a relationship to bloom and flourish without care and attention.

If you want to protect the love you have and see it continue to flourish, then spend time in doing the things that will allow it to get back to that place.

Put effort into creating fresh experiences, the time together, the admiration and the longing that gives love the special power and attraction that it holds for us.

Realize the special characteristics of the love you already have in this moment and take time to appreciate it, honor it and invest your own time in it by planning special times or organizing events and trips. Invest practical time and emotional energy in what will create mutual respect, understanding and ongoing love as you move forward together.

9

SIMPLE SELF HELP

You are in control

The old saying goes *"If it's to be, it's up to me."* I think nowadays that it should perhaps also say *"If it's to be, it's up to you too!"*

No matter what life throws at you, good or bad, how you respond is something you have total control over.

There is nothing in your life that you cannot change, that you cannot act upon, that you are unable to see in a different light and take some level of action about.

No matter how difficult the situation is that you find yourself in, regardless of any negativity that you live with daily, and in spite of some temporary destructive environment that you may be experiencing right now, there is a better place for you along with better opportunities. It is simply that they are just beyond your current ability to see them.

Change your way of looking at the actual challenges that face you. Acknowledge them. You must do this or you will be in denial. But don't look at them as cast in stone, as something permanent or fixed or as the only single reality there is. You have to see that these circumstances can be changed and that you can make progress beyond them. No part of who you are is so fixed that you cannot create a different and better set of circumstances.

Of course, there is choice and you are the one person that gets to do the choosing. There is no reason for you to settle in the place of second best or to allow bad situations to persist in damaging aspects of your life. Instead, identify the ideal picture of how good you wish that thing to be, of the way that a certain outcome might change so many things for the better.

The first requirement is that you recognize what it is that you have and be firm about what you do not want, about what is dysfunctional or that does not serve you in any positive way. Be clear that you are willing to let these non-beneficial things and circumstances go.

We could be talking about a clunker of a car, of a distressing home situation, of a distorted relationship, of a job or workplace where you experience inappropriate behavior or plain bad practice. You may want to break free from a crippling cycle of debt or from a relationship where there is neither love nor scope for change. It might be that you are in a place of personal despair and lack hope.

Begin to make a shift in your situation by stating clearly that you no longer want to put up with any of the things that you have considered and which you have written down on a list. By getting to a state of clarity about the things that you do not want you are at the same time creating more space for the right things, the right people and the right circumstances to come into your life.

So start with identifying what you *don't* want.

Now move quickly and clearly into what you *do* want. Enjoy describing the detail of what you want, and go to work on the process of asking the world to provide you with these.

The Universe likes a person to ask clearly for what they want as it then has clear instructions on what to do and will always work at providing you with what you ask for. If you make your list and do the asking and what turns up seems at odds with what you asked for, rather than blame the Universe for giving you the wrong stuff, first check what you asked for. So often people will think they asked for X when actually they asked for Y and a bit of something else, or for Y with a little distortion. When you get something that seems different you should always check the original list you were working from!

Do those things that will take you closer to your goal of creating, attracting and then receiving the life that you wish to experience.

Remember that making choices is about deciding from a set of those things you do or do not want, from a choice between what calls your attention or what propels you in a different direction and towards something else.

Making choices is also about coming up with some detail so that you are not just guessing.

Sometimes you will need to expend energy in work or labor towards a goal. At other times the goods will be delivered to you almost instantaneously by your wish for their existence.

In each case the deciding factor is the detail that you put into your request and the choices that you make from the options available to you. The biggest mistake would be to think that your choices are limited when, in fact, they are abundant.

When things are going the way you want, remember that you are in control. And do not forget that when things are *not* going the way you want them to, that you are also in control!

Choices

Moment by moment and one day at a time, your life is happening. And at the same speed your life is passing by. You can end up looking back over your shoulder at the life you might have had, should have had, or could have had if you had only just got on with it. And how would you have done this differently? I'll tell you how. Moment by moment and one day at a time is how!

This is all you have, the now, this moment.

There is nothing else outside of this moment in which I am sitting here writing, late at night in a quiet room while the world sleeps around me. And you out there somewhere, reading these words on a screen or on a printed page in the very moment that is your own NOW moment.

So we must make some decisions, you and I. Another word for Decisions is Choice. The Choice to move forward with our lives in this moment. Do we turn left or right at this junction of the roads, at this crossing of paths? It is a bit like the way that you take your first footsteps as an infant. You do not know that you will be walking in the future, but you do sense that the next thing to do is put the other foot forward, and then the other, until it happens and you are walking! But you started with the next foot. Choice always begins with a simple action. Not with a complicated, philosophical, much thought about action. Instead you just did *something*. From this you get first one result and then another.

Most of the choices you have made have not been monumental in their significance. They have been ordinary, mundane and habitual. Yet in this very normal state your choices take you to some quite extraordinary places. They put you with amazing and wonderful people, allow you to experience the highs and lows that life will deliver.

Without action and movement and the flow of energy that comes from choices, what is there ? Nothing. Inactivity, lack of movement, zero forward motion, only stagnation. From such a place nothing much can come. But even the decision to stay down there is a choice.

So you see you always come back to the point that in order to nurture yourself with Simple Self Help, to attract the people, the opportunities and the feelings that you desire, you have to wholeheartedly engage in making choices. Moment by moment and day by day.

Change happens

Life is not necessarily always going to run along smoothly, and there will understandably be times when you want to shout out loud: *"Stop the world. I want to get off."* We have all been there at some point in our lives. I am a big believer that we are here to learn the things, to understand the concepts and to appreciate the belief systems that surround us. The more I think about this, the simpler it is to get the point that change happens for a reason!

If you are in denial about change, or regret that it happens, then you are potentially just setting yourself up for more disappointment, frustration and anger, and also for more lost opportunity. Instead, you could choose to realize that change is actually one of the few constants around us. Yes, this might sound bizarre, that *"change is one of the few constants",* but it is very much this way.

By acknowledging this change conversation you open yourself up to the possibility of greater opportunity, stronger experiences and less upheaval by embracing instead of denying change. You will also very likely receive more of what you expect that is good and positive.

When a career stops short of the time that you had expected to be protected by it, when a business folds or requires you to stretch beyond your normal habits, when a relationship arrives seemingly from out of nowhere, how will you be prepared for it? Will you have thought through the potential outcomes and communicated this quickly to the place marked 'Beneficial Change', or will you instead be looking to the place marked 'Change for Changes' Sake' or perhaps 'Change without obvious Benefit?'

Embrace change. Allow it to happen and then respond with what you need to do. It might be to ignore the change until the timing is better for you to understand it, but you have to see that it is happening to you and let that recognition carry you through to new and better circumstances that will follow just as day follows night.

Attracting the best results

At all times you are drawing to you those things that happen around you. No exceptions! So if the life you have does not reflect the life you want then you really need to do something about it, and fast.

One sure way to step closer to the results you want is to acknowledge what is going right for you, to identify and give thanks for the things that are working, for those areas where you are pleased and be happy with what you have in the moment. The act of showing gratitude will cause more of the same to come to you.

Give attention, focus and energy to the practical and logical aspects of attracting the results you want. How are the parameters of your work defined? Who are the people you know who can help you in determining the outcomes that you want? Have you shared with them the detail of what you seek to bring about with their help? Aside from the people you know, who else might be out there in the wider community who could be beneficial for you if only you could make contact with them?

Put some thought into describing the people and the physical resources and materials that will take you toward the results that you want. Consider the scope for you to tell people as you meet with them about what you want to create.

Remember that the Universe will always give you what you ask for and, with this being the case, you need to be clear that you are asking for what you want to receive. Only ask for that which you really want. The alternative is to ask for that which would be okay or acceptable or reasonable. The issue in this case would be that the Universe does not know which is truly great or magnificent or fabulous. But you do know the difference and so you need to ask for the outcomes you want to see turn up in your life.

If you will just let it, then life will always seek to astound you with what it delivers up for you.

Create a Vision Board or a Treasure Map of what you want. From your favorite magazines, books and social posts, clip the images and ideas that fill you with inspiration and motivation. The involvement of more of your senses will serve to accelerate the process of attracting the good that you deserve. From the websites and catalogues that have products and offerings that you love, cut the images that mean something special to you. Pin or paste these onto your Treasure Map, placing the images in such a way that they call to you and encourage you in the pursuit of your goals.

Continue to believe in your own ability to create the results that you seek.

Vision and values

Creating the life you want and producing the results that matter to you is about ensuring you are clear on the values by which you live and lead that same life. If you expect challenges you may get them. If you anticipate a bed of roses and an easy walk through the park, it is likely you will get this, or something akin to it. Develop the focus that supports you.

Your vision and the values by which you lead your life each day are crucial in underpinning the results you get and the actions you go through in order to create the results you want.

If the vision you have is a measure of the breadth of your ambition then expanding your vision is likely to have a corresponding impact on the results that you achieve. Tied in very closely with this is the matter of the values that you embrace and live with as you pursue your vision of a life that truly reflects not only what you want, but also who you are.

The values you hold might be such things as honesty, hard work, thrift, balance, happiness, friendship, trust, self-discipline and others. Each one that you identify and adopt for yourself is a piece of the jigsaw that is you. In the same way that principles are timeless, so too are values. These values act as a benchmark by which you can judge and assess not just the progress that you are making towards your goals, but also serve to help you measure yourself against colleagues and friends, clients, relatives and family members. Not as a benchmark of things, but more a yardstick of characteristics and values you admire.

In your own life there will of course be times when the principles and values that you live by will be tested. Equally, you will discover time and again that the more you lead a life in which your vision and values are in alignment together, you will receive rewards and pleasures unheard of by those who do not understand. Hold to what you know and feel to be right.

About the author

Collector of books, fan of new reading and ever fascinated with the power of the written world to bring new ideas and thinking.

As an author I love time spent at my desk in my dedicated writing shed at the bottom of the garden or at a table in a neighbourhood coffee shop. I love to be with pens and paper working through ideas for a manuscript or a presentation.

Best of all is getting a concept out of my head and into a conversation with a reader, discussing our different ways of approaching something which unites all of us. This could be around Financial Thinking and Personal Budgeting, dealing with the Clutter we accumulate in our living spaces or wanting solutions and new ways of thinking about Debt so that we can enjoy more control of our money on the way to financial peace of mind.

It is so great to do what I enjoy with the writing, getting good feedback for the books that people enjoy and which can be seen to be making a positive difference.

Nick Sturgeon
Find Nick at www.nicksturgeonbooks.com

Sign up

Sign up to Nick's Newsletter for the latest news about his books, subscriber-exclusive offers and freebies. It's absolutely free and you can unsubscribe at any time.

To sign up, go to: nicksturgeonbooks.com/signup

Printed in Great Britain
by Amazon